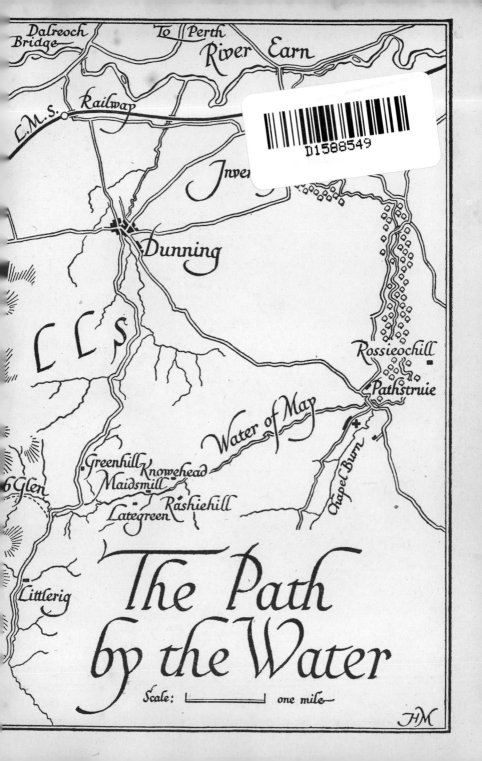

The Path
by the Water

Scale: |⎯⎯⎯⎯⎯| one mile

Dalreoch Bridge • To Perth • River Earn • L.M.S. • Railway • Inve... • Dunning • L L s • Rossieochill • Pathstruie • Water of Map • Greenhill • Knowehead • Maidsmill • Rashiehill • Lategreen • Chapel Burn • Glen • Littlerig • HM

THE PATH BY THE WATER

By the same Author
BY MANY WATERS

First published November 1944

THE PATH
BY THE WATER

A. R. B. HALDANE

Wood Engravings by Helen Monro

THOMAS NELSON AND SONS LTD
LONDON EDINBURGH PARIS MELBOURNE
TORONTO AND NEW YORK

To the Memory of
MY MOTHER
whose love and understanding
made so easy and so pleasant
my path by the water

PREFACE

In the pages which follow I have made an attempt to recall and describe certain portions of my childhood from the earliest days I can remember up to the age of eighteen. The path has led for much of the way by the waterside and these chapters may be regarded as describing the early education of an angler. But in looking back over these years I realize that the process of education by burn, loch, and river has not been in fishing alone.

There is, I think, something to be gained for each of us if we turn now and then to look back over the way by which we have come, no matter how undistinguished that way has been. Much which had been half forgotten comes back to the memory ; something, too, of the meaning of past happenings and of their influence on our lives may come to us, giving us an insight into the trend of our path and some small added knowledge of ourselves.

So, just as among the hills at home I have sometimes turned for a moment from my fishing to look back down the glen up which I have climbed, I have in these pages sought to retrace in recollection stretches of the path from childhood to early manhood, and since fishing has at all times been my passion and my chief delight, the backward glance has lit on much of wayside detail in those years through which continuously the fisherman's path has led. I have seen in retrospect the pools and streams by which I once stood, have felt the freshness of the grassy hills and uplands over which I once passed, and have known again the thrill of the black water and the mystery of the overhanging banks. I have felt the roughness of my worm tin and known the taste of home-made food, and from them my mind has recalled much of my home surroundings and the figures of those who often accompanied and always helped me.

From the earliest days recalled comes little but the recollection of growing keenness to catch trout and the thrill roused by their capture. Later came a consciousness of the wild life and the flowers and plants of the waterside, the mimulus and mint beside which I dropped the worm or cast the fly, the trails of woodruff and forget-me-not hanging to the water. With stronger legs and wider range came a fuller knowledge of my surroundings and the realization that the richness of wild life and natural growth, which hitherto I had seen only in isolated and unconnected detail, all went to make up a perfect whole ; and from this gradually came something more. As time went on, I found that every now and then I experienced sudden and intense waves of feeling induced most often by some unexpected view, but sometimes by nothing more than these same small details of flower, plant, or animal life, and occasionally by the mere memory of something seen or experienced on other days.

To attempt to analyse these feelings is quite beyond my power. I can only describe them as feelings of complete and unquestioning assurance coming from the conviction that beauty in Nature is ultimate and abiding ; that having seen it and known, if only for fleeting and infrequent moments, the emotions which it can arouse, we shall somehow one day share in it and in those things for which it stands.

These are things which we see only dimly and understand imperfectly. We see them " as a shepherd boy far away among his hills might see the glittering of the army of a great King, and he is awed by the majesty and bows low at the vision of greatness and dreams over it when the army is passed and he turns to his humble task with his sheep."

Moments such as these have not come only by the waterside, but nowhere else have they come so frequently. In few places is the wealth and beauty of Nature more richly scattered. When there is added the happiness which fishing brings to the fisherman, it is not surprising if the times of most intense feeling have for him been experienced beside the water. So it has been with me, and for this reason I think that such small widening of perception as has gradually come to me has come at times and in surroundings such as I have tried to describe in these chapters from the early history of a trout fisher.

EDINBURGH, *June* 1944.   A. R. B. H.

CONTENTS

FIRST BEGINNING

" From quiet homes and first beginning
Out to the undiscovered ends. . . ."

A LITTLE way before it reaches Stirling the road by which the traveller approaches the town from the south passes over a shoulder of rising ground. The view from the top is a striking one. In the middle distance lies the old grey town, the houses clustered round the foot of its hill and then rising tier upon tier as they climb the rocky shoulder, from the top of which the castle looks out north and west to the blue edge of the distant Grampians. Farther to the east, the waters of the Forth, already tidal, wind slowly down through flat ground gradually broadening out to the Firth. Beyond the river on its north side is more flat ground for a little way, till suddenly the line of the Ochils rises abruptly from the plain, a line which extends north and east for thirty miles to the Estuary of the Tay and the borders of Fife. This south face of the Ochils is very steep, and looking at them from the road which follows close at their foot one is reminded of the abrupt rise of the Alps from the Valley of the Rhône as it flows down to the Lake of Geneva.

From the valley of the Forth the hills rise through wooded slopes, then to shoulders of bare hillside where rocky outcrops break through the white bents, and so on up to the summit, which at the highest point of the ridge is over 2,300 feet. Here, on the south side, the burns come down the hill face in steep rocky courses, and though I do not doubt that there are trout far up many of them, they can hardly be said to lend themselves to trout fishing. But if you cross the ridge or circle the hills to their north side where my home is, you will find that the precipitous rise of the south face has its counterpart in a much gentler slope, and this is one of the reasons why the north side of the Ochils forms an almost perfect environment for the early fishing days of a child. For here the hills lie back quietly and at their ease, rising fold on fold and shoulder beyond shoulder, leading one on by gradual steps and stages till the highest point is reached several miles back from the main valleys of Strathallan and Strathearn, across which the Ochils face the Grampians.

Nature has given the Ochils a plentiful water supply from springs which come out of the hill face far up, under swelling cushions of quaking green turf on which you step at your peril, or in open springs bubbling up into small pools of clear cold water through sand and fine gravel in which the little water insects burrow. These springs seldom go dry even in the driest summer, and though most of them are so small that you would hardly expect to catch trout immediately below them, I know one at least which must almost rival in size the great springs at the head of the chalk streams of the English downland. Each fold in the hills has its spring at the far end under the final steep rise to the ultimate ridge, and in addition there are usually on the sides of the surrounding shoulders smaller springs all draining into the little glen.

The brown trout of the hill burns is content with a small pool in which to live—in fact I think he often prefers it if it has a stone or an overhanging bank under which he can retire if need be—so it is not many yards before the stream formed by the joining of the overflow from these springs is big enough to provide a home for him. The gradual slope of the hills results in a stream which, while it moves freely and briskly in little runs and tiny falls, seldom goes headlong, and so although there are a few burns near my home where larger falls bar trout from access to their top pools, in most cases a trout can climb to the point where the supply of water and the size of the pools is no longer sufficient even for his modest needs.

In my early days I was fortunate in living surrounded by these friendly hills and within easy walking distance of a number of small burns full of brown trout, and to the opportunity for fishing was added the incentive of the example and keenness of others. My elder brother Pat, seven years ahead of me, was already a keen fisherman. So too, almost more important in my very early days, was our nurse who, as she often reminds me, came to the family a few months before I did, and who for my first few years was my chief fishing companion and instructor. In this my good fortune was and still is far beyond the ordinary ; for Nurse is of that fast-dwindling number of nannies most often found in, or at least hailing from the north, who give many years and sometimes their whole lives to the care through childhood and beyond of those fortunate children entrusted to them. There was, too, Speed the keeper, a devoted man, downright and out-spoken, with a genius for direct and sincere comment whether complimentary to the object or otherwise, who took it for granted that fishing and shooting were among man's chief ends. So had I failed to develop an interest in fishing, it would not have been for lack of example, encouragement and opportunity. At what stage this interest first began to show itself I do not know, but it must have been very early in my life, for looking back now I cannot recall a time when I did not have a desire to fish.

Behind Foswell our house, an old grass road leads back into the hills. If you follow it for a few hundred yards, you come to a place where beside a single birch tree it splits into two. One branch leads through whins and scattered larch trees to the foot of the heather and on towards the high slopes of the hills, to lose itself eventually in the bents near the top, 1,500 feet above Strathearn. It was down this road in the old days that the tenants of the farms on the lower ground, of which our home was originally one, brought the peat which at that time was regularly cut, though peat burning is now practically unknown in the Ochils. The other branch of the road leads on and eventually joins the old road over the hills to Glendevon, a drove road of much importance in days past, but now for most of its length grass-grown and deserted. Following this second branch of the road, you cross a small burn and in a few yards come to the keeper's house at Bells-hill, once a small farm, where the byre and stable of the original steading are now used to house ferrets and rabbit traps and dogs with young pups temporarily moved from the kennel to the warmth of hay-filled stalls.

Not far from the keeper's house, and just back from the burn, is a small pond only a few yards across, used in the old days to drive the mill, the last remnants of which were still visible at the burnside when I was a boy. So far up in the hills, it is not now easy to see where grain could have been profitably grown, and it may be that the mill was used rather for beating flax after it had been steeped in the pools of the near-by burn. For in the old days flax was a much commoner crop than it is now, and even far up in the hills beside crofts and small farms the blue and the white flowers of the slender plant must have been a familiar sight.

Since then the pond has fulfilled many functions, including its present one of acting as a link in a hydro-electric system, and in the early days of which I write it played a very important part in my life. It was full of trout, and I had discovered that they would take a worm, if given a sufficiently long time to think about it. I had not, then, the patience to wait for the trout, so evening after evening Nurse and I would attach a worm to the line on the bamboo cane which was my rod, and throw the bait out into the pond, laying the cane on the grass weighted with a stone, to take its chance through the night.

At this time, during the summer preceding my fifth birthday, I had in the mornings some elementary form of lessons from the governess who taught my brothers and sister during the spring and early summer, and I remember the ill-concealed impatience with which I waited till midday. Then, my lessons over for the day, I was free to slip from my seat at the table in the corner of the dining-room which was our schoolroom. Snatching a biscuit from the brown cupboard outside the pantry door, I would hurry off with Nurse up the Bellshill road between the beds of hemlock and the wayside clumps of broom, and so to the pond to discover the result of the night's fishing. It was a shameless process and not too humane, and the only plea in mitigation which can be offered is that it gave me enormous pleasure at a time when I was hardly old enough even to fish the little burn beside the pond.

So far as I can recall, we found a trout on the line most mornings, with a regularity which I hailed with joy and regarded without suspicion, but which I have since come to think was not unconnected with the activities of Speed, who, while professing contempt and indignation, saw to it at least that the supply of trout in the pond was replenished from the burn, if indeed his intervention was not even more direct.

It was not very long before the time came when I started fishing the small burn which ran just below the pond and from which the pond was fed. I still used the six-foot bamboo cane which was my first rod ; indeed, I continued to use it for several years, and on these little hill burns it had many advantages over more orthodox but less-easily handled rods. Where the small burn flowed past the pond it ran among whin bushes growing on a bank covered with blaeberry plants. I have reason to remember the whins, for sometimes when lifting a trout from the water, swinging it round sideways as one should do, or jerking it over my head as I was apt to do in the excitement, I would find it in a whin bush behind me,

5

and no-one who has tried to deal with a small wriggling trout still on the line, which has fallen through the top of a close-set whin bush, will wonder at the clearness of my memory.

Above the whins, the burn ran through a small gully among scattered larch trees, and here some of the pools had got partly filled with fallen branches, so that there was a great chance of an active trout grabbing the worm and being able to retire among the sticks under the water, when the hook was almost sure to be caught up as you tried to pull it out. Here were no nice overhanging banks for the worm to float under, and so though there were plenty of trout, I much preferred the part above, before the burn entered the trees and where it ran among rushes, the open hill on both sides and the heather coming almost down to the water. Up here among the rushes and grass the burn was very small. Now and then would come a pool where there was perhaps a breadth of a yard of open water into which to drop the worm, but this was the exception, and often the stream would quite disappear as the overhanging banks came together, while the grasses on either side interlaced. Then, all one could do was to look for a space, it might be a yard or two upstream, where a gap in the grass enabled the worm to be dropped into the water. When this had been done the line was slackened, allowing the current to carry it downstream or under the banks as far as it would go.

These were most productive spots, and time and again in such a place I would see and feel the line dragged suddenly to one side, sometimes with the sound of commotion in the water as an eager trout dashed out from under the bank. There was no question of waiting to strike. I found that these little trout were very quick to take the worm and to eject the hook by some devilish cunning which ensured its becoming caught under the bank, when I was forced to lie on my stomach groping under the turf edge to release it, my head overhanging the frightening blackness of the little pool. The only plan was to strike as soon as you knew the worm had been taken, and, if possible, to do so with a sideways movement so that the trout was pulled out from under the bank, keeping it clear of the lip of the overhanging turf.

Fishing like this was very slow work. The burn twisted about in the rushes, and if the trout were taking well or on the frequent days when they seemed to acquire a special instinct for taking and ejecting the hook with no worm on it, one covered little ground. But then the whole scale of the operations was small. The rushes among which one guided the worm had then for me almost the significance of trees, while the small stones round or below which one strove to float it seemed as large and important as great boulders are to a salmon fisher on a big river. So it was not surprising that a few hundred yards at most sufficed me for several hours, and the top part of the burn, where it turned farther into the hills and at last reached a point beyond which no trout could go, remained a little-known country reserved for very occasional longer expeditions.

Looking back on those early childhood days at Foswell, certain backgrounds appear and recur constantly as settings for the pictures recalled to mind of our life and activities. There is, I think, in us all, at least in childhood, a natural tendency to turn again and again to surroundings which by reason of their ease of access, their beauty, or some undefined and unsuspected quality appeal to the imagination and give us a sense of security and pleasure. Such a place for us was the burn and the little pond by the keeper's house. On hot afternoons in July we bathed in the pond, afternoons which must have been times of alarm for the trout, for the pond was small, and except for one big boulder behind which most of my nightly catches were made, there was little cover.

The burn, too, served a double function in our lives, and there are still places where you can see the traces of the dams which we made partly with a view to making bigger pools for the trout, but more often, I think, just for the pleasure of seeing the water rise while we hurried to add turf and stones for the support of the banks against the increasing pressure. We got very hot and wet and dirty, and few of the dams which we constructed with such care and labour survived the winter floods, but it was a favourite ploy and one which never lost its attraction. Sometimes in moving stones from the near-by

7

bed of the stream to complete the dam, we would come on a small trout living in one of the few holes which Nurse and I in our frequent fishings had not discovered, and then dam-building was abandoned while we " guddled " for it, and having caught it, put it into some tiny pool until the dam was finished and ready to receive its first occupant. Our dams were not always on the burn itself, for there were hollows here and there along its banks where in the old days the flax was laid to steep, and these too we sometimes made into ponds, leading the water to them in little tracks from the burn.

Below the keeper's house the ground became steeper, and on this part of the burn was a little waterfall pool. This I fished again and again, and it seemed to have some of the qualities of the widow's cruse, for the supply of small trout seemed inexhaustible, nor do I think that in this case Speed was responsible for the continuance of the supply. I daresay one explanation was that it could be fished only from a high bank above the water and a hooked trout had to be hoisted up from water level, a process during which, I fancy, the hold of the hook often gave way, giving me ultimately the impression of repeated catches while in fact making comparatively small inroads on the population of the pool.

To-day the small glen is planted with Scots firs and spruces through which the stream tunnels its way unseen and only faintly heard from outside the wood. Its character is quite changed with the disappearance of the grass and rushes and ferns which once covered its banks, but the pools are still clear in my mind's eye : the deep pool in the narrow cleft of the rocks, which one could fish while keeping entirely hidden ; another under overhanging whins ; a stream running in be-tween the stems and whitened roots of the willows which grew at the side of the burn under an old larch tree.

A few yards farther and the burn took a great leap over a sheer fall thirty or forty feet high. This was called Connel's Spout, to commemorate the man who once lived in what is now the keeper's house eking out, it is said, a hard and bare existence on the croft by illicit distilling in a still cunningly hidden under the roots of a big elm tree on the bank of the burn. A steep path led down to the foot of the fall, where little waves lapped the edge of the wide circular pool into which the water fell. If the burn were running full, the falling water would shoot far out from the top of the rock to fall past dripping ferns and moss on the cliff face in a great cascade of white. Then the dappled brown of the pool's surface was almost hidden in the white tumbled water and the whole of the hollow around the pool was filled with spray. The noise in that space under the rock face and the overhanging trees was deafening, and climbing back up the steep path after fishing the pool I would hurry to escape from the frightening volume of sound which seemed to envelop and enclose me, breathing again more freely as I reached the turn in the path half-way up where the noise suddenly became less and the wind in the trees and the sounds of the friendly world outside were heard again.

Sometimes if the burn was not in spate, or its sound had not driven me back up the path, I would fish on down below the pool. Here the steep sides of the glen were covered with a tangle of hazel undergrowth, while here and there were small ledges of close-bitten turf where the rabbits sat. A little farther and the burn came again to the edge of a steep cliff face down which it fell to join a larger stream in the main glen below. But here in the early years I never followed it. Instead I would turn aside at the birch tree whose trunk was blackened by the smoke of many picnics, and so along the wood path under the laburnums, through the gap in the holly hedge, and home.

CHAPTER II

FARTHER AFIELD

I HAVE mentioned two of the allies or accomplices who helped and encouraged my earliest fishing—Nurse, and Speed the keeper ; but there were others who readily gave their help. Those were days long before I dreamt of fishing with anything other than a worm, nor would it have been possible with the garden cane I used, to cast a fly. The very first stage in my fishing expeditions was, therefore, the collecting of worms, and here James McEwan, the old gardener, came to my help. My demands on his time must often have interfered badly with his morning work of taking vegetables in to the cook, but he was never too busy to come with me, bringing his spade or a three-pronged fork which in the north we know as a " graip."

Sometimes we did our digging in a part of the outer garden where round the cold frames the big leaves of the rhubarb which grew behind the lavender beds kept the soil always moist and soft, sometimes near the bed of mint in the corner of the inner garden or between the gooseberry bushes and the raspberry canes, one of which latter I remember grew a particularly luscious variety of yellow rasp. McEwan, hissing softly through his teeth like the old coachman he was, dug, while I knelt beside him ready to pounce on the worms as he turned the soil, for they were wary and very active in getting back into their tunnels in the ground. These worms I collected in an empty baking-powder tin, supplied by my friend Annie the cook, in the bottom of which I had put a small cushion of moss.

When he was tired of digging, McEwan would sometimes drive the graip deep into the ground and shake the handle vigorously backwards and forwards, a manœuvre which always had the effect of making the worms emerge hurriedly from the soil, though whether from fright or curiosity I never knew.

McEwan was himself a keen fisherman, though it was only sometimes in the long summer evenings that he had time to fish, and I would consult him as to which burn I should try. I regarded him, and he certainly regarded himself, as something of an oracle. Indeed, few people dared contradict him or question his superior knowledge on almost any subject. He himself used to tell with complete gravity and serious satisfaction that on one occasion when a former employer had complained that while flowers planted by McEwan grew, those planted by himself did not, he had replied, " Ye see, sir, I pit mine in richt end dounmost."

As time passed and my tin grew full and the delay in the morning's work serious, McEwan would straighten himself from his digging, and wiping his moist nose on the back of an earthy hand would remark that if I brought home a trout for every worm I would do well. I can see him now, standing outside his tool shed with folded arms, his trousers baggy and darned at the knees from constant kneeling by flower beds, the sleeves of his thick grey flannel shirt rolled up to the elbows showing the brown weather-beaten skin of his freckled forearms, the grey side-whiskers framing the rosy cheeks, the straight upper lip and the fine aquiline nose. Few gardens and few stables can have known a finer face or a kinder man.

Then there was Annie the cook, grey haired and short sighted. Her functions as a friend and ally in my early fishing days were rather less obvious and direct than those of McEwan and Nurse, but none the less important. Her sandwiches and rock-cakes filled my pockets on the more distant expeditions, and it was she who in the evening held the ashet, as we call a large plate in Scotland, on which the catch was piled, or fetched the weighing machine on the rare occasions when the size of a trout justified its use. On a shelf in the big store-cupboard in the servants' hall near the kitchen stood two great paper bags, one of golden sultanas and one of currants, and Annie closed her already short-sighted eyes to the frequent raids which I made to eke out my lunch thrusting my hand deep into the soft sticky mass of the succulent sultanas or among the dry sweet currants.

Towards the end of July when our late-ripening strawberries were picked, the kitchen was filled with the warm sweet smell of the jam-making, and as it boiled and seethed in the great copper pans Annie would skim off the sweet pink froth, ladling it into cups and saucers from which we supped it. Sometimes I would come into the kitchen to find her rolling out or cutting into shapes for firing luscious if indigestible mixtures for cakes or scones or pastry, and then she would give me little corners to nibble, or cut out a cake or scone of unusual size or curious shape for my own special benefit later at tea in the nursery upstairs.

Looking back on those days, I wonder whether I realized at all how much I owed to Annie, for unofficial and smuggled delicacies, for tolerance of unpunctual meals, for kindness at every turn. I wish it were possible to tell her that now I do ; to tell her that half the fun of the last quarter mile down the Bellshill road from the hill after fishing was the prospect of clattering down the steep stairs into the warm appetizing smell of the kitchen where she, leaving her cooking, would hurry off to fetch an ashet, beaming and exclaiming over the catch with a pleasure which kindness made, I believe, almost as great as my own.

In front of our house, facing north to the valley, was a narrow strip of gravel and mown grass ending in an herbaceous border and a terrace, beyond which rough natural turf sloped down to the tennis lawn fifty feet lower. A narrow grass path led down the slope to the lawn, and on either side was a thick round clump of rhododendrons, full of nests in spring and a safe refuge for the rabbits which the efforts of Speed and McEwan never quite succeeded in keeping outside the wire netting surrounding the garden.

Every autumn for many years my Mother had planted daffodils on the slope. They had spread and increased, till more and more each spring one seemed to look down from the house over a sea of white and yellow. First came the big single trumpet daffodils, the simplest and the best of all, then a more slender and taller variety with white petals and pale lemon-coloured centres, and last, near the end of May, the

Pheasant's Eye narcissus whose thick petals surround with silvery whiteness a heart of yellow with crinkly edging of red.

Near the top of the path, and growing in the rough grass on either side, were fritillaries, some cream coloured and some of the mottled purple kind which seem more at home in the rich meadows beside the Thames below Oxford. The rough ground on the slope was left uncut, and as the spring went on it became a race between the late flowering Pheasant's Eyes and the new grass pushing up. For a few days, the white blossoms showed through the heads of the shooting grasses, but then they started to fade and soon the whole slope below the house was covered with a sea of waving grass which bent and swayed in the wind.

After the main hay-cutting was over, Speed and two of the farm men would come with scythes, and for a day or two they were at work cutting the long grass round the house, partly for the sake of the natural hay for Major the cob, which they made into little springy haycocks, on which we bounced and played, but more to prevent the coarser grasses from ripening and seeding. The scything was no easy job, for the grass on the slope grew from a deep bed of moss and lichen which caught and smothered and turned the point of the scythe. Now, when I recall those July days, there come to my mind the sweet smell of new-cut hay drifting in to us at our lessons through the open windows of the dining-room, the sound of the men's voices as they worked and the steady rhythmic brush of stone on metal as one after another they paused to sharpen with rough whetstones the edges of scythes blunted by the strong coarse grass.

As the work went on many things came to light—a mouse's nest of dried grass, a sodden tennis ball lost weeks before, once a willow warbler's nest hollowed into the moss of the bank, and every year two or three wasps' nests. Some of these last were in holes in the ground but others hung from the branches of the rhododendrons and trees under which the scythes swept. Every year Speed and his men got stung and came to the laundry window for washing blue where the kindly Agnes, through the steam of her wash-tubs, ministered to their wants with ready sympathy. The nests in the ground rather defeated us, though we did our best to deal with them by pouring tar into the holes, but the hanging ones were easier, for at night when the wasps were inside they could be set on fire with burning tow on the end of long sticks. The young wasps while still in the grub stage were good bait when used on a fly, or as an addition to a worm, but one had to be careful when collecting the comb that no adult wasps were still on it, and once a wasp hatched out while the comb was in my worm tin and crawled out fully fledged and far from pleased when I removed the lid.

Foswell is built into the side of a steep hill, the ground rising so quickly behind the house that after climbing the stair which leads from the hall to the first floor you can walk out from that floor on ground level to the back of the house and the stable yard. Here in a low pink-harled outbuilding was the gun-room where hung my fishing-basket, except when Nurse in the interests of hygiene washed it and hung it to dry among the Gloire de Dijon roses which covered the walls and which blossomed all through the summer and on till the late autumn. From the gun-room, having collected my lunch from Annie and slung the basket on my back, I would set out, saying over to myself lest I forget anything :

> " Hook, book, basket ;
> Rod, reel, flasket ; "

the last item covering a packet of sandwiches, a couple of thick biscuits stamped with the name of the local baker, and one of Annie's rock-cakes. I can hear now the musical tinkle of my worm tin rolling about in my basket as I hurried up the road to the hills, or down to the burn in the glen.

Through the wooded glen below Foswell runs a burn rather bigger than the one by the keeper's house, which ultimately joins it, but still only of a size to be fished with a worm on a short line manœuvred carefully among the trees, and here, as my fishing took me rather farther afield, I often went. The best way to reach it was to follow down the steep road which climbs to Foswell, past the big cherry tree which in early summer becomes a mass of little white hanging globes, and the patch of blackthorn where once I found a lesser redpole's nest. The blackthorn looks across a meadow to a sandy knoll where rabbits sit and sun and scratch themselves among the broom round the mouths of their holes.

Near the place where the burn comes out of the glen and passes off our ground, the road crosses it by means of a stone bridge. Beside the bridge a tiny whitewashed cottage looks across the stream to a line of walnut trees bent and leaning with age, whose leaves I liked to pick and crush for the sake of their sweet aromatic scent, the only smell I know reminding me of the scent of bog-myrtle. The little cottage dates from the days long before the coming of housing regulations. It was a minute building long since fallen into lamentable condition, where tramps and casual farm workers occasionally camped in summer. I used to think of it as the house of gingerbread and sugar which Hänsel and Gretel found in the forest, and the bedraggled and ragged old men whom one sometimes saw emerging from the door did nothing to dispel my childish fear that it was the house of a witch.

Fishing up the burn, one came first to the sawmill, and if one were lucky and the men were sawing, there would be a fine head of water from the dam far above coming out from the tail race of the turbine and filling the burn below. Here was the clean smell of sawn wood and sawdust, and of creosote from the big tank which stood in the corner of the shed where a tree-creeper used to nest. Above the sawmill the wood thickened, hanging in places over the water, and here a nicely balanced mixture of speed and caution was called for. One had to strike quickly before the trout could get one tied up among the sticks at the side of the pool, but if one struck too hard, or unsuccessfully, the line often flew up to become entangled in an overhanging branch from which there was little hope of detaching it.

Half a mile up the glen was the dam which stored water for driving the sawmill and for making electric current for Cloan, my uncle's house. The dam was full of trout which accumulated from the burn above, and in summer when the water was low one could see them very clearly; but it was quite useless to try to catch them with a worm, while the surrounding trees and the absence of ripple made it such a difficult place to fish that even later on when I had acquired some facility for casting a fly, I seldom got many. When the water level in the dam rose to the lip of the spillway, it over-flowed down a steep face of concrete which flattened out into a smooth broad slab over which the water ran, to fall eventually into a large pool at the foot. Here in the autumn spates the sea-trout would congregate, and when the burn was in flood we loved to watch them jumping on to the concrete slab and wriggling their way up to where the slope became too steep for them and they were washed back into the pool. We often tried to get in behind them with a landing-net, but once headed downstream they were wonderfully agile and strong even on the concrete, and we seldom caught any. It was here on a November afternoon that I came on the only otter which I have ever seen near my home. The sea-trout were running at the time, and it had no doubt followed them up from the distant river in the valley to the dam where I found it swimming.

The other great excitement which the dam afforded us was when once a year in early summer the men opened the sluice and ran off the water to wash away the mud which had collected during the previous winter, and which after a time seriously reduced the storage capacity. We would wait at the outflow of the sluice with nets till the flow of the water had almost stopped, and then for a halcyon few minutes there was an almost solid stream of trout. I must add in mitigation of this that the majority of these we put into pails and took up again to the burn above, a very necessary precaution, for the thick mud washing down the burn would otherwise have choked them, a fate which I am afraid must in any event have overtaken many in the pools immediately below.

Above the dam, the burn bent and turned among the oaks and the ash trees and the firs of the glen. Sometimes it ran beneath overhanging alder bushes, now it hurried and splashed among stones as it washed the base of a mossy wall, and now it ran slow and deep at the bends where the current had eaten under the roots of the trees, forming dark holes where the trout lived protected by tangled bunches of sticks and leaves.

It is, I think, characteristic of a child's imagination that the world for him is divided into isolated regions of thought and experience. Each has its own peculiar quality of form, colour and sensation, and seldom does one of them bear close relationship to another. In a world whose bounds are so restricted as they must be in childhood, these regions are often in close proximity to one another, so that within quite a short space—it may be by crossing a path or rounding the corner of a hedge—a child may pass as if over an unseen frontier from one land to another.

The early days I spent at Foswell provide many examples of this. At one end of the strip of mown grass in front of the house which looks down to the tennis lawn grows a weeping ash. Its branches growing from the upper part of the trunk arch over to hang trailing to the ground on every side and earning for the tree the name " Umbrella Tree " which we gave it. In summer the space so enclosed round the trunk became a green chamber ten feet high, hidden by the leaves from the outside world and carpeted with deep grass where McEwan's mowing-machine did not reach. Here we sat, read, played shops or made bows and arrows in our little world hidden and apart.

The " Umbrella Tree " had for us a character and feeling and atmosphere of its own, and so had the long line of thick laurels on the west side of the house where we searched for green-linnets' nests, trying sometimes to climb from end to end of the line without once putting a foot on the ground. Then there was the well surrounded by ferns, the overflow of which fed a square concrete pool where we paddled and sailed boats or occasionally kept newts and small trout. Close by it, a great circular slab of stone five feet across, the grind-stone from some old corn-mill, rested on a thick cut from the trunk of a larch tree to form a table, and here, when a more distant picnic was impossible, we often took our tea.

Finally, in a place apart and above all the others, was the nursery, smelling of scrubbed cork-carpet, oil lamps and tweed coats ; a friendly, homely smell. Nurse sat by the low window sewing and darning our clothes, the floor round her pitted deep with impressions in the soft floor-covering from the castors of the armchair which held her comforting bulk. Above the table a long single shelf high on the wall held among a miscellaneous collection the animal books of Thompson Seton and William J. Long, with *Little Women* and the three volumes whose pages record *What Katy Did*. Across the room a mirror over the fireplace was flanked by tall vases standing at either end of the mantelpiece. These contained bunches of feathers stolen one by one and often forcibly from the peacock at my uncle's house across the glen, till at a later stage Nurse removed them lest they prejudice the matrimonial prospects of the family.

Of all these places so close to one another I thought as distinct and complete little worlds, within rather than part of the larger world of childhood. The burns too had for me the same feeling of individuality, and within a short radius of our house were several which though very close to one another, produced in me entirely different reactions. Even now, walking beside them, I find I can sometimes recall the different trains of thought which they started and even the tunes I whistled or hummed beside them. This was true not only of different burns, but sometimes even of different parts of the same burn.

The burn in the wooded glen which I have tried to describe was divided in my mind into two distinct parts—divided so sharply that even now I still find myself thinking of it as two burns. The dividing line was a very clear one. Following the burn upstream one came to a point where it suddenly emerged from the trees and came out into a small meadow. Even its name changed here, for above the trees it was always locally known by the name of the occupant for the time being of the little whitewashed croft on the shoulder of the hill below which it ran. Above the meadow willow bushes grew overhanging many of the pools. One deep pool I remember especially, which I used to try hurriedly and half-heartedly, torn between a fisherman's keenness, and anxiety lest my line get entangled in the underwater roots of a willow bush or its overhanging branches, involving a scramble down the steep bank to the very edge of the deep water, a prospect which filled me with alarm.

Next came a deep gully with thick ferns and bracken on the slopes above, and rock roses among the boulders of the steeper parts. Beyond that was the open hill with the burn running through rushes in a tiny glen typical of those of which the Ochils have so many. On either side the slopes of the glen rose so steeply that in places tiny landslides had left bare tracks of red clay and trails of stones where butterwort grew and down which in wet weather the water dripped and trickled. In other less steep places the sides were covered with coarse grass and bent, beneath whose overhanging tufts were favourite places for nests of meadow pipit and yellowhammer. Beyond these steep banks, the hill sloped up more gradually to the white bents of the high shoulders where patches of rushes, among which the blackgame sat, hid the vivid green carpets of moss round the springs which at intervals fed the burn from either side.

Few of these little side streams were more than the merest trickles, but there were two in which just before they met the main burn there were little deep pools almost hidden in the grass and rushes, where trout could be caught. The remnants of an old dry-stone dyke ran up the bottom of the glen, and as the burn wound its way from side to side, it continually crossed and recrossed the line of the dyke whose stones had in places slipped down and lay covered with moss and weed forming splendid cover for the trout. To the curlew which soared high overhead, the little glen must have seemed a bright green track winding down through the white and paler green of the bent-covered hills. In early summer, the sides of the stream and the stones were thick with forget-me-not, and watercress and mint grew in beds in some of the quieter pools. The short grass on either side where the sheep liked to graze was full of wild white clover, and later in the year the turf was sprinkled over with the yellow-gold stars of tormentil.

The burn had all the features for which the trout of the Ochils look. There were weed-covered stones for them to lie behind ; there were overhanging banks concealing deep safe hiding-holes running far back under the turf ; there were little quiet corners out of the stream on whose surfaces water-spiders performed their curious antics and where insects dropped off the ends of overhanging grass and rushes, and there were sudden little slopes down which the water poured in swift smooth cascades over long trails of the dark green weed where the fresh-water shrimps live.

I have fished this burn in all weathers, when the water was bright and clear, when it was full and tinged with brown, and when it was in roaring spate. Of all the burns near home it has seemed to me the friendliest, the quietest and the best, and of all the trout I caught in the early years, the greater part must have come from it. They were fat little trout, short and thick and stocky, some of them almost a little hump-backed as if from the cramped quarters under the banks of the tiny pools in which they lived. The higher up the burn one went the darker in colour the trout became, and from some of the smallest pools where the banks nearly met over the water, I have pulled out trout almost completely black except for the vivid red spots on their sides and the hint of dusty gold on their gill-covers and round their eyes. The water of these Ochil burns is not very peaty, and I have often thought that the extreme blackness of these trout came less from this than from the fact that their whole life is spent far back under an overhanging turf bank, their only movement a dash out from its shelter to grab a passing shrimp or worm, their only link with the outside world the sound of a ewe grazing on the turf above them.

The head of the burn lies close in under the hill where the ground rises steeply to the bog on the top of the ridge. Here is a small waterfall, and when I first knew the burn it seemed to form a barrier beyond which no fish could go. One year we took up an old water-can from Foswell, and filling it with water transported above the fall a half-dozen trout from below. There for a year or two we left them in peace to breed and increase. Later we fished for them in the few fishable pools above the fall. I remember feeling rather half-hearted about wanting to catch them again, and I cannot recall that we did in fact get any ; but one of the shepherds later told me he had seen them in the pools, so I hope and expect that they or their descendants are still there.

Last autumn I walked up the little glen looking for black game in the rushes. A little way below the fall I crossed the stream, which was at that time low and clear, and as I did so noticed in the pool a good-sized trout. I followed up the burn to see whether there were others, and in the waterfall pool came on another lying motionless just below where the dwindling stream splashed down from the lip of the rock above. He seemed a trout of nearly half a pound, a heavy weight for these hill burns, probably an old fish which had lived quiet and unmolested in that pool for many seasons, for it is years since I last fished the pool, and I do not think that many others go there. I left him undisturbed, planning and hoping to go there and fish for him some other day.

CHAPTER III

COULSHILL

AS time passed, my fishing education passed with it from the hands of Nurse to those of my elder brother Pat, and from now on a growing part of each summer holiday was spent with him beside such of the burns round Foswell as were within my walking powers. Our usual plan was to start fishing upstream from a point a mile or two from the top of the burn where the pools were large enough for fly to be used. My brother would fish a little way ahead with fly, while I lagged behind, trying with a worm under the banks and between the main pools where it was impossible to cast a fly.

Such a division of the fishing was sensible and logical, for in this way each of us used the method best suited to his capacities and experience, while we held the theory, borne out in practice, that fly fishing disturbed the pools less than bait fishing, the rod coming behind having thus a fair chance of getting trout. For all that, in the lower parts where the stream was big enough for fly, I had at first little hope. The pools seemed very big and broad for my small rod, and I missed the overhanging banks and the rushes which to some extent made up for my inexperience and lack of patience. Though my brother would often leave a pool only half fished and in moving to the next kept far back from the bank to avoid disturbing the small holes and corners where I would have my best chance, I fished half-heartedly with one eye on him, ready to run up and overtake him should I see him catch a trout. I was not sorry when lunch time came and we sat on the bank where I emptied out his basket, counting over again and again and arranging in order of size the trout he had caught and adding my own meagre contribution.

As we fished up the burn the pools grew smaller, the banks closed in, and I felt more confident. My brother took off his fly cast and put on bait, and from then on we fished alternate

23

pools on an equality. For while I still lacked his experience and patience, I soon came to know where to fish, and just as a boy often develops a genius for finding birds' nests, so I acquired at last a sort of instinct which told me the most likely places for trout.

Gradually with experience I came to know something of the real art of burn fishing. I learned how to fish holes and corners of the pools beyond the length of my rod, by swinging the bait like a pendulum so that extra length could be gained without the sudden jerk which would have detached the soft worm. I learned to search most carefully the tiny backwaters beside the run at the neck of the pool, along the edge of the foam which after rain lined the banks, and the corners where little cakes of froth, richly browned by the flood water, spun round in the eddies. I learned to put the worm accurately into the narrow strip of water between the main current and the bank where the stream flowed more gently. Here an inch or two one way or other might decide whether it was caught by the current and swept downstream, or lingered drifting in the stiller water, tempting a trout to dash from the depths of his hole under the turf and grab the bait with a movement often so quick as to defeat the eye. I came to know that if the worm stuck momentarily on grass or rush, a gentle pull would often free it, so that it fell into the pool beneath. This was a most effective method, and indeed in worm fishing, and later in wet and dry-fly fishing, I have often had cause to rejoice in the irresistible attraction for a trout of a fly or bait so presented.

Bitter experience came to me, too, of days when cunning trout nibbled off the worm and departed undetected and unscathed, or other days when trout too small to keep swallowed it so deeply that I had to kill them before with difficulty extracting the hooks. From this I learned that the fisherman must by constant gentle and tentative raising of the rod top keep in touch with his bait to get early knowledge if a trout should take it. My earliest years with the garden cane had implanted in me the bad habit of jerking the trout from the water, a method abrupt and uncompromising, and one which allowed for little modification to meet varying circumstances. Now at last, armed with a three-piece Greenheart rod, I learned to temper my keenness with discretion, allowing the spring of the rod top to help in pulling the trout from under the bank.

For the young fisherman, the day on which he first starts to fish with a fly marks, though he may not know it, his entrance into a world of sport of which the horizons have at one bound receded and widened to unimagined distances. Hitherto his fishing has been limited to the small burns, or the head waters of the larger ones, his hopes and fears, doubts and expectations, on a scale corresponding to the proportions of the little world in which he moves. If he is wise, he neither forgets nor discards the friendly intimacy of the small burns and their trout, for in present experience or later retrospect there can be few things more pleasant, but to this has been added a new world of interest and enjoyment unfolding before him in lengthening and widening vistas of days to come.

Our memories play queer tricks on us, recording vividly and indelibly scenes and episodes apparently trifling in their nature and significance while passing over others of which in later days we recognize the importance and which we long to recall. It is therefore with feelings of regret rather than surprise that I realize my total inability to remember the day I first fished with a fly. But while I find it impossible to recall with any accuracy when this occurred, I am in no doubt as to where I made my first attempts at fly fishing.

Beyond the keeper's house at Bellshill and past the pond which saw my earliest fishing, an old grass road keeps to the side of the hill looking down to the larches and oaks of the glen below. On the road itself, the ground has been pressed smooth and firm by the passing of horses and carts in years long past, and later by the feet of shepherd, keeper and postman. Here the grass grows rich and sweet, covering the ruts made by the traffic of bygone days and sprinkled through with wild white clover, but on either side the turf of the hillside is poor and dry and mossy.

Below the road the ground falls steeply to the glen, and on the slope in June are great patches of wild pansies, yellow and purple. Around them a spreading carpet of woodruff grows so profusely that from a little distance the turf seems powdered with snow dotted with pansies and sprinkled over with a star dust of yellow tormentil. I suppose there is no one of the paths in the hills at home along which I have passed so often with rod and fishing-basket as this old track, for it leads to the upper part of the burn in the glen, and beyond this to the larger stream where I first used a fly.

Across the glen on the opposite hillside, a farm road runs parallel to the grass track. Soon the two roads join, and from the gate where they meet you look up into the broad quiet glen of Coulshill. Grassy hills dotted here and there with clumps of whin and round patches of bracken rise on either side, steep on the east side but more gradual on the west, sloping and climbing back to the distant skyline, while at the far end of the glen a steep wall of hill blocks the view beyond the head of the burn. In the cup of the glen beside the burn is the farmhouse of Coulshill. Its harled gable-end looks north over the black-currant bushes and lupins of the garden, and behind the house the steading and sheep fanks run part of the way up the hill.

At the foot of Coulshill glen where the road begins to climb, it passes close beside a group of old ash trees standing round scattered piles of stones half hidden in deep rank grass. We used to be told that long ago in the house which once stood among the trees a murder had been committed, and on a misty autumn day there is still something rather sinister about these stones and the great trees, whose roots and branches have grown with age into shapes as grotesque and suggestive as any in Arthur Rackham's pictures. But now hoodie crows nest there, and in May and June there is often a cuckoo calling from the trees, while sometimes you will find Highland cattle and their cross-bred calves standing or lying among them, contemplative and contented.

Shortly before you reach the farm, a very small burn, the first of three which feed the main stream, passes under the road. On the lower side is a small pool into which the stream falls when it emerges from the little tunnel taking it under the road.

26

Early in the year the pool is open, but as the summer goes on, the meadowsweet on the bank grows up, wild mint appears among the stones at the sides, and the pool shrinks till only a tiny patch of open water is left. When I came to it on my way to fish the Coulshill burn, I always used to try it as a matter of course, and as I had usually a fly cast on my rod in preparation for fishing the main burn, I would let this dangle over the roadside fence and " dap " the tail fly on the pool. With so little open water it was a difficult business to avoid catching the meadowsweet at the sides, and long grass and harebells which grew out from the stonework of the bridge did not improve matters. But I never thought of leaving that pool untried, and came to look on the result of my efforts in it as a sort of omen of whether or not I should have a good day. Quite often a trout would dash out from under the banks which overhung the neck of the pool and take the dangling fly, when a quick heave would land it wriggling and jumping in the dust of the road beside me.

A few yards below this pool this little stream joins the main burn, which, shaded by ash trees and willows, runs at the foot of a steep bank sloping up to the edge of the farm-house garden. In March and April the bank is sprinkled with scattered clumps of snowdrops jettisoned at some time from the garden above, while the catkins on the willows are powdered with yellow pollen among which on mild days the first bees search hopefully. Later, in June, the banks of the burn and the whole of the little bit of meadow ground which stretches upstream for twenty or thirty yards, becomes a mass of wild geranium growing so thickly that for a time there is little green to be seen, only a great sheet of purple.

Beyond the house at Coulshill the road turns in to the farm steading, crossing the burn on a high stone bridge. Ivy covers the parapet, but on the steep bank of the burn on either side under the bridge a mass of periwinkle falls to the water and hangs, trailing its long shoots in the current. As you stand on the bridge and face upstream, you look up a little gorge where the burn tumbles over big boulders and rocky ledges overhung by old ash trees whose branches grow out over the stream.

Immediately above the bridge is a long pool. The water falls into it over a ledge of rock and the force of the current has made a pot-hole where the water swirls and eddies before it flows out into the smoother part of the pool which stretches down to and under the bridge. If you look from the bridge down into the neck of the pool where the deep water of the pot-hole under the shade of the trees is dappled green and brown, you will find that the reflections at first defeat your vision, but every now and then you will get a glimpse down to the rock in the bed of the stream and at such times you will often catch a glimpse of a trout swaying and drifting with the current as it watches for food washed down by the stream. It is not possible to cast a fly into this broken water, but I used often to try to drop one on to the trout which lay in the tail of the pool under the bridge, though here too overhanging branches often led to disaster.

Such were the surroundings of the place where I first learned to throw a fly. It was not an easy school, for there were few places where from bank to bank the stream was more than a few feet across and fewer still where the channel was not broken up by moss-covered stones or rough out-crops from the rock which in many places formed the bed of the stream. Stunted willows grew over many of the deep holes and backwaters where the trout lay and on either bank grew tall grasses bending over the water, or beds of bracken, all ready to trap a badly aimed cast and to hold it so firmly and inextricably that it seemed that Nature had designed them for no other purpose. It often happened that even an accurate cast suffered the same fate, for the wind which blows in these winding glens and gullies of the hills seldom blows steadily, and a sudden puff or an unlooked-for lull would land the flies several feet from the water among a tangle of bracken and rushes. Here, too, growing experience gradually came to my aid. I learned to know by the look of the grass or the feel of the line whether a sharp tug would free it, whether to lay down the rod and crawl forward to disentangle the line at the risk of scaring the trout, or whether to abandon the pool. Many a time I have been driven to this last resort, venting my

childish temper by tearing to pieces the offending frond of
bracken. There was one other alternative, for if the line
were hopelessly caught but the pool too good to abandon or
risk disturbing, I would sometimes break the gut deliberately,
tying on a new fly and chancing being able to find the broken
end of gut when the pool had been fished. But this was a
desperate expedient and one to be adopted only in very
special circumstances.

The burn at Coulshill taught me many things besides
accuracy in casting, lessons repeated and emphasized on other
burns among the hills at home. From painful experience
with waterside bracken and grass and rushes came at last the
realization that the use of more than two flies merely increased to little purpose the risk of tangles and other disasters.
I came, indeed, to know that in places where the pools were
very small and much overgrown, it sometimes paid to use only
one fly, a practice which I would have applied more generally
on the burns but for the obvious and peculiar attraction to the
trout of the second fly dangling and bobbing on the surface.

In thinking of these burns and visualizing their pools and
streams, I find that generally I trace them with the mind's
eye upstream to their source. There are many who think
that a stream should always be fished in this way, for the
reason that the trout lies facing upstream and so is more easily
approached unseen from below. Except in dry-fly fishing,
I have never been convinced that this plan is the best, and in
practice I fished either up or downstream according as the
one method or the other happened to suit the plan of the day's
expedition or the direction of the wind. It seemed to me then,
as it still seems, that each had its advantages and attractions.
When I fished upstream I found it easier to pull out of the
water small rising trout, a trick which, as time went on, I
found could be brought to a point where, if the effort were
well timed, one could be reasonably sure of jerking the trout
back to where one stood, and even sometimes of catching it in
mid-air. But far better than this, the upstream burn fisher
faces into the hills, the stream before him a track of silver and
green leading him on and up into the quietness.

But downstream fishing, too, had its advantages. One cast less frequently, the current straightened and tightened the line, while the flies, drawn slowly upstream, could be guided far more accurately between boulders, close in to the side of overhanging bushes or up into the little eddies under the bank at the neck of the pool, the single dropper bobbing against the stream. This latter advantage was an important one. In the burns of the Ochils the deepest parts of the pools generally lie up near the neck on either side of the rush of the stream as it enters. These deep quiet corners are small in extent and very narrow. If one fished the pool from below in the ortho-dox way one might, by a combination of luck and skill, place the cast so that the tail fly fell into the quiet water ; but this called for very great care in casting, and, no matter how skil-fully one cast, it was impossible to keep the fly in the quiet water for any length of time, or to prevent it being quickly caught up in the main current and swept back downstream. So I formed the habit, even when following the burn upstream, of walking round many of the pools and fishing from the neck down, unless the wind, or the pool's shape, made this im-possible. I learned to draw the cast right up, sometimes almost under my very feet, and often, having learned the importance of the dropper fly, I would stoop or kneel in order to lower the rod and keep the dropper on the surface for as long as possible. It always seemed to me that not only did this method offer the best chance of getting trout, but that the bob of the dangling fly on the surface tended to attract the best and most vigorous trout, just as I believe a floating fly attracts better fish than a sunk one.

There was, also, another advantage. These burn trout, and perhaps especially the smaller ones, seem in summer to lie perpetually on the look-out for flies, and there are days when the fall of the flies on the surface and the rise of the trout to them are almost simultaneous. Such fish are hard to hook. Eye, hand and mind must, in a flash, change from a downward throw to an upward lift, a sudden reversal which it is not easy to accomplish quickly and smoothly. When the cast is first made, too, the rod point is low and the risk of snapping the

gut as one lifts it suddenly to strike a rising trout is correspondingly increased. But as the cast is pulled upstream, and the rod
point rises from the water, the risks of breakage decrease ; the
line is shortened and gathered in the left hand ; the dropper
trails and then hangs dangling and bobbing on the surface
as it is guided towards the fisherman, crossing or lingering in
tiny bays and eddies and corners of quiet water tempting the
trout from beneath the overhanging banks.

The typical rise of a trout to a fly so worked is not the headlong splash of a fish out in the body of the pool. It is rather
a quiet head and tail rise, or a little leap into the air at the
hanging fly. I used to think of such rises as the deliberate
calculated rises of feeding trout rather than the impetuous
indiscretion of youngsters ; and even when such trout, rising
close under the bank, were lightly hooked, the hold was often
sufficient to allow one to jerk them the few feet necessary to
land them on the turf of the bank so close above. Then if
the fly came away, I would drop the rod and rush forward to
grab the trout as it kicked and wriggled down the sloping bank
to home and safety. Sometimes my hands were stiff and
useless with cold and wet, or cramped with the tight grip on
the rod's handle, and time and again trout, slipping from
between my fingers, were retrieved at the eleventh hour by a
foot hastily thrust between them and the water, perhaps only
to be lost in the end.

The trout at Coulshill taught me many other lessons. Some
I learned consciously and later tried to apply deliberately,
while there were, I do not doubt, others which I learned
without being aware of it, and many which I have yet to learn.
I learned to detect the rise of a trout through the sparkle and
glitter of broken running water, whether it was the head and
tail rise of the fish which breaks the surface, the flash of one
which turns below it, or only the sudden check of the line.
But especially I learned to fish most carefully the quiet water
along the very edge of the banks. To-day when in retrospect
I recall these burns, I see the little narrow pools, full and
clearing after a spate, the quiet eddies by either bank where
the grass, still wet and glistening with the night's rain, bends

31

almost to the surface of the water, and the brown and gold flash of a trout rising head and tail to the Greenwell's Glory as it trails and hops upstream against the current, gay, tempting and provocative.

It was hardly to be expected that in these small hill burns trout of any great size were to be found. From the time I first started fishing up till the end of the last war, there was a period of ten or twelve years during which in my holidays I was seldom away from the burns, and during this time I believe I acquired as intimate and detailed knowledge of them and the trout in them as one could well hope to have.

Looking back, I must admit that few of the trout which I caught—and not even many of those I lost—stand out in memory as having been of any great size. Now and then my fishing diary records that of a number caught in the burns on some particular day, a few were " big ones," but I see that reference to their exact weight is discreetly omitted and I have a strong impression that my use of the term " big one " has been generous. Most of the trout I caught were pulled out of the water, often violently and without any preliminary play, and many of those caught on fly were actually jerked back to me as I stood well back from the pools. The small lifting capacity of a whippy Greenheart rod and still more the breaking strain of light gut when subjected to sudden violent stresses, indicates that few of these trout can have been much over four ounces, an estimate which corresponds with my memory of them. A few were certainly heavier and I can remember some which were played carefully and landed in my bare hand, a perilous proceeding in the small pools whose sides were generally overhung with grass and bracken and rushes. But by far the most must have been trout of from two to three ounces, and looking back at my memory pictures of the glistening piles of brown and red and gold heaped so often on the ashet in the Foswell kitchen, I fancy I can see few larger.

I have sometimes wondered that the trout did not grow larger, for the fresh-water shrimps which they love flourish among the gravel and weed of these burns. But surface feeding is scarce, the bitter cold of the winters on the high ground must check all forms of insect life, and it is probable that the whole food supply is barely sufficient for the comparatively large population of the pools. That this is at least part of the explanation of the small size of the trout seems to me to be shown by one incident. The dipping tank for the sheep at Coulshill is built on the hillside immediately above the farm steading, the ground sloping from it down to the burn. Each season after the dippings, it was the practice of the shepherd to drain off the residue of used dip so that it seeped through the ground and became relatively harmless before it reached the burn. But one year owing to a sudden flood of rain or some such mischance, the strong poison of the dip found its way directly and undiluted into the burn, with the result that for some way below Coulshill the greater part of the trout were killed. For the next few seasons that part of the burn had few fish in it, but those that remained profiting, I imagine, from less keen competition for the available food, grew to be noticeably above the usual size. What these burn trout lacked in size, however, they made up in numbers, and though I never achieved the great baskets of past years of which Speed and McEwan used to tell me, I see in my diary that catches of forty to sixty trout in a day are quite often recorded.

Above the trees which surround the bridge at Coulshill you come out into a little piece of upland meadow ground at the foot of which the burn runs in streams and little falls, with good pools between. In June on the drier parts of the meadow overlooking the stream grow quantities of a flower known locally as " bald mingie " or St. Baldred's money, though I think the full name is *Meum Athamanticum*. Its flowers are like small cream-coloured cow parsley, the buds and stems tinged with pink, the sweet-smelling foliage a delicate green, soft and feathery as asparagus fern. It is a flower fanciful in its choice of surroundings and seldom have I seen it elsewhere than on ground sloping down to a burnside in these hill meadows of the Ochils, sharing a dry sunny bank with the harebell, the lady's bedstraw and the thyme.

As you climb by the burn through the meadow, you pass a marshy patch where ragged robin and later grass of

Meum Athamanticum

34

parnassus grow, and a thicket of willow where the fleecy down of the early blossom used by the nesting pipits drifts with every puff of breeze. Then comes a long still pool at the head of which the water pours in a tiny fall under a water-gate let into the drystone dyke which marks the beginning of the open hill ground. Ferns grow on the bank, and if it is June the pale green leaves like bishop's croziers will be half uncurled from their brown fibre coverings and the short grass beside the pool will be scattered with tormentils.

Beyond the dyke is the open hill. Up the slopes in summer are stretches of bracken, dark shiny green, its solid masses thinning gradually as it climbs the hill for a few hundred feet, beyond which the white bents stretch on to the summit. A little way above the water-gate the stream passes through a narrow cut in rocks which rise sheer on either side thirty feet above the black surface of a deep pool whose waters never see the sun. At the top of the cut the gap separating the lips of the two rock faces is only a few feet across, and they say that in the old days a sheep stealer with a ewe on his back leaped the cut and so defeated his pursuers who were afraid to risk a fall to the black pool below. The big hole between the rocks is full of trout which you can see from the tail of the pool if the light is right, but to throw a fly into it means a difficult sideways cast. It needs some patience and perseverance, but is by no means impossible, and we used to get many trout out of that pool, though never the monster which I know lives in it. Even if the trout failed, there were as the summer went on large juicy blaeberries to be had, for the blaeberry plant loves a rocky ledge overhanging water where the berries are safe from the grouse and the blackgame which feed on them where they grow on the open hillside.

For some way above Coulshill, the burn is large enough to be fished with a fly if it is cast lightly and accurately with a steady hand, but after a time the main burn is joined by a side stream which comes in on the west side, and above this it is too small for fly. The side stream comes tumbling down from the hill, crossed just before it reaches the main burn by an old stone bridge carrying a grass-grown track which has been running parallel with the burn all the way from the farm. The track is wet and boggy in parts and there are places where in the storms of past winters torrents of water have rushed down it and torn up the surface, leaving great holes and trails of rough stones ; but it shows all the signs of having once been a carefully made road, for this was at one time one of the principal roads leading across the Ochils. By it in the eighteenth century, great droves of small black cattle from the Highland glens were driven to Falkirk Tryst and other cattle markets in the south, and later it was a carriage road continuing to be used till a comparatively late date, perhaps to avoid the toll on the better road up Gleneagles or the Blaeberry Toll on the road which crosses the hills behind Dunning.

Beside the bridge is one of the coldest and strongest of all the many good springs in the Ochils. It bubbles up from a sandy bed in a little pool under a rock, and as you lie with your face over the water to drink you will see the sand stirred into constant motion by the force of the rising water. The spring is well placed, for immediately beyond it the road starts to climb steeply, the frequent bends still faintly visible in the grass showing where in the old days the horses dragging the coaches up felt the slope. The road bears a little to the west, and after many bends and turns reaches the top of the hill in a slight dip beyond which begins the descent to Glendevon.

Here on the skyline is the boundary fence of the farm, and where it crosses the road is an old wooden gate with a wicket beside it. It is known as the " Cadger's Yett," which means the Pedlar's Gate. When I was small, I used to picture fierce terrifying men with thick sticks and few scruples striding over the hill to overtake me in the half dark. Now I think rather of some old man who has perhaps trudged these hills for many years reaching the gate from the Glendevon side. Before starting down towards Coulshill he stops, like Matthew Arnold's " Scholar Gypsy," to rest leaning on the spars of the gate ; and indeed he could choose no better spot, for here is no sound but the call of plover and curlew, or the

sound of the wind in the grass. From the gate one looks north over Strathearn to the line of the Grampians from Ben Ledi and Stuc-a-chroin to where in the east the hills tail off in blue distance to the Angus glens ; and but for the shepherd's house at Coulshill far below there is no sign of man or habitation till one looks over the wide valley and sees, if it be evening, the far lights of Crieff.

At the junction of the two burns, I take off the cast with the partridge spider on the tail and the Greenwell's Glory as the single dropper, and putting on a short bait cast and a small Stewart Tackle, fish on upstream with a worm. The stream bends and twists, overgrown and almost hidden by the rushes and grass of its tiny strip of meadow ground beyond which are steep slopes covered with deep moss and ferns, and then the more gradual slope of the hillside up to the skyline. From the rushes mallard often rise and an occasional grey hen, and right up at the far end of the glen a hen pheasant each year nests and rears her family. Here at the top of the burn you stand almost ringed in by hills rising in front and on both sides. On them you can make almost a complete circuit of the glen, keeping always to the top of the ridge and walking the whole way through bents, bleached to silver white by the sun and the wind.

One windy cloudless day in early September I climbed the slope above Coulshill farm, crossed the drystone dyke which marks the beginning of the outer hill, and followed up the bank of a little side stream to its spring among thick

rushes on the face of the hill. Beyond the rushes I climbed on
through bents up the hillside and came out at last on the
flat top of the ridge. Behind me the ground fell steeply to
the Coulshill burn from which I had climbed and beyond
which to the south-west were mile upon mile of grass and
bracken and rushes. Facing me far to the north were the
Grampians, Ben-y-gloe, Ben Vrackie and the high ground
round Glen Tilt, while nearer were the screes of Craig Rossie
and the Pictish encampment above the rocks of Ben Affray.
At my feet, the hill sloped down gradually to a burn beyond
the ridge. The bents waved in the north wind, and standing
there with the wind on my face and my feet deep in the
moving grass, I seemed to stand on the sea's edge facing an
incoming tide. The little waves came dark up the hillside
before the wind to sweep over my feet, and turning I watched
them, a hundred ripples changed to silver, going from me over
the summit into the sunlight.

CHAPTER IV

THE LOCH AT FOSWELL

A SHORT way back into the hills behind our house was a piece of soft boggy ground where mallard nested in early spring and snipe were often shot in autumn. It lay in a saddle, on one side whins sloping up to heather and on the other a grassy hill with old Scots firs growing on its top. The bog covered the water-shed, and from one end the water drained north-west straight down to Strathearn, while from the other it flowed south to feed the small burn which ran near the keeper's house, finally reaching the valley of the Earn rather farther to the east.

In 1908 my father and my brothers had the idea of making the bog into a small loch, and I remember watching them taking rough measurements with the aid of a spirit level laid on the barrel of a shot-gun to determine where the banks would require to be placed and the approximate area of water which would be enclosed. The site seemed a curious one, the ground falling at both ends, and the supply of spring water from the bog itself being insufficient, it was necessary to provide for water being led in a ditch round the hillside from the small burn near by. But all these difficulties were found to be capable of solution and eventually a local contractor set to work to construct the banks.

All that summer and autumn the work went on, and by early spring the loch was complete and filling gradually while we remained happily ignorant of the fact that owing to the use by the contractor of an inaccurate level, one bank was in the centre appreciably lower than the other. It so happened that as the water level neared its highest point, a big snowfall occurred followed by sudden heavy rain, with the result that much surface water was added to the normal intake to the filling loch. The water rose suddenly, reached and over-flowed the top of the low bank, while a strong east wind added to the danger. Early one morning we were roused by the news that the loch had burst, pouring down into the valley and sweeping away trees and bridges, but mercifully hurting no-one.

Later that day we gazed on the ruin of six months' work. A clean-cut gap thirty feet wide had been broken in the bank of the loch, and through this the water had burst. From the nature of the damage done, it seemed that the column of water had not spread out sideways but had largely retained its initial shape, with the result that the damage was restricted to a narrow belt within which the water had cut far into the ground, tearing and gouging long trough-like holes many feet deep. The worst of the damage was on our own land, so serious complications were avoided. The bank was securely rebuilt, the loch refilled and the damaged ground planted with young trees in narrow strips which in their early years formed admirable nesting ground for partridges. Now after thirty years these have developed into belts of well-grown trees, almost the only places on the estate where one has a reasonable chance of cornering a cock pheasant.

Meantime a supply of young trout for stocking the new loch had arrived from the hatchery at Howietoun. Indeed, by some curious freak of Fortune they arrived in the afternoon of the day the loch burst and consequently had to be put into the little pond at Bellshill. In these cramped quarters they remained for several months, and as the natural feeding of the pond was not nearly sufficient for so many, they were fed from the banks each day with minced rabbit and similar delicacies. This made them very tame and unsuspicious, and if one approached the bank they would swim into the shallow water at the side, waiting in an expectant shoal for the worms which we often threw to them between their regular feeding times.

Such a trusting frame of mind threw a considerable strain on my sense of honesty, and all things considered I record with some complacency that only on one occasion, returning from an unproductive afternoon at the burns, did I fall to the temptation of throwing a baited hook among the waiting crowd. The capture which inevitably followed profited me little, for the size and marking of these Loch Leven trout were so distinctive that my catch could not be taken home to proclaim aloud its origin among the smaller and more homely occupants of my basket. Instead it had to be hastily thrown back into the water, while the troubles of conscience lingered on to torment me long after the victim itself had lived down the memory and effect of the episode.

The day came at last when the loch was full again and the young trout were transferred in cans and pails up the hill to their new home. We knew that the flooding of the ground and the subsequent rotting of the surface vegetation would produce an ample food supply for the trout for several years, during which period we could look for their rapid growth. To improve the position still further and to provide food later on after the first richness of the early years had passed, we sank at various shallow points in the loch round baskets containing roots of lakewort, a useful food-producing water plant which covers the bottom in the shallows like a great lawn of lush grass, giving when the light strikes it, a lovely tint of green gleaming through the golden brown of sunlit water. We made small piles of stones in the shallows, too, and among them we put hundreds of little fresh-water snails, while in the ditch bringing the water to the loch we planted watercress from the burn and other water weeds among which live the fresh-water shrimps which form an important part of a trout's food.

It was an exciting day when we first fished the loch in the

spring of the year after it was stocked. The trout which we had put in were mostly two-year-olds, so that by the following year they should have grown to be fish of half to three-quarters of a pound ; and so in fact they had, but the very first trout I caught out of it must have been one which had found its way down from the burn, for the first entry in the fishing register which we kept records in my elder brother's handwriting that my capture weighed " .01 oz." and " gave a lot of play ! "

During the next few years our experience of the growth of the trout followed very much the lines which are familiar to others who have made and stocked lochs in similar ground. By the end of the fourth year, the average weight had grown to fully three-quarters of a pound and the trout were in splendid condition. For a few years they kept round about the same average weight, but gradually the influx of native brown trout from the burn above which we could not entirely prevent, and the breeding of the loch trout in and round the mouth of the intake led to overstocking and the average size began to fall. Subsequently we made several efforts to reduce the numbers by heavy fishing and netting, but in the making of the loch the contractors had dug clay from the bottom leaving deep holes which defeated all efforts to net effectively, while the growth of weeds and rushes added to the difficulties. So with the exception of a few good seasons, and particularly one when the average rather inexplicably rose to nearly a pound, the average weight of the trout has fallen to about half a pound, though every season a few much heavier ones are caught.

During the years which followed the making of the loch, it became increasingly a centre of interest and affection in our life at Foswell. The footpath to it across the shoulder of the hill grew more and more clearly marked in the short grass. Reeds and ferns, willows and yellow flags took root and grew along the waterside, hiding the lines of the artificial banks, while the young trees planted all round grew and gave it their shelter. To-day I find it impossible to visualize the place as it was before the water was there, nor can I imagine, so essential a part of our life at Foswell did it become, what we should have done without it.

During the loch's existence, there can be few circumstances of time, of season, or of weather in which I have not seen it. I have seen it in late March when a hard cold wind blew from the east, bringing the smell of burning grass from the hills behind Dunning, when the young larches on the hill above showed as yet no speck of green and only the frogs croaking in the shallows and the plover calling over their nesting ground told one that " the hounds of spring are on winter's traces " ; on long summer evenings when it seemed that if one climbed the hill above the loch one would see the sun barely dipped behind the Grampians ; on autumn days of wind and rain from the south-west, or winter evenings when the smoky orange and pink of the sky was reflected in patches of smooth grey ice which the wind had swept clear of the snow lying powdered and crusted on the frozen surface.

Of all the times and seasons, two stand out and colour most often the pictures of the loch which come to me. The one is a morning in late July or early August. In these months more even than in autumn we get in the Ochils mists creeping in the evening up Strathearn from the Tay estuary, or dropping down on the hill tops as the clouds tire and drift to rest. By morning Foswell is lost in dense mist. Only the distant sound of a goods train climbing the long incline from Perth comes up from the valley to link us with the world, while in the dry depths of the dripping laurels the sparrows congregate, their chatter subdued by the heavy white stillness of the world outside. It seems that the sun can never get through the thick moist vapour, but by eleven o'clock there comes through the white a tinge of gold. Now you can make out the shapes of the rhododendron clumps on the slope below the house and soon you can see down to the tennis lawn. Then the sun breaks through, overwhelming and devouring the shreds and rags of the mist now drifting in helpless defeat, and the sparrows in a rising storm of cheerful gossip adjourn their meeting and fly off in ones and twos on the business of the day.

On such a morning I would take my rod and net and set off up the old road behind the house, past the poplar tree at the gate with its leaves hanging limp with scarcely a tremor, between the tall beds of hemlock on the roadside and past the single bush of sweet briar which grows at the bend in the road and which has to my knowledge survived now for thirty years the repeated loss of its leaves crushed in my hand for its scent as I go to my fishing.

Where the path to the loch strikes up the hillside, it passes through an expanse of that short grass common in old pasture on high ground, whose head is a delicate network of tiny pinkish brown seeds set on the points of slender stalks. From a little distance it almost seems that the ground is covered with a gauzy film of brown. On dewy mornings, or in misty weather, each little seed holds a minute bead of moisture, adding a silver sprinkling to the haze of brown and lightly showering a thousand tiny drops as one passes through it. Mist still lies drifting over the tops of the oak trees in the glen below and there is no ripple on the loch's surface. Trout are rising freely, some jumping and splashing but a few feeding more quietly, hardly breaking the calm, for after a morning of mist the sun brings out flies on the water.

It seems a shame to launch the boat and break such quiet and its ripple may disturb the rising trout. I used often to find that the most effective plan, and one which suited best the stillness, was to push the boat out from the boat-house and after rowing a few strokes to let her drift on slowly and then sit quietly waiting for feeding trout to rise within casting distance. I found, too, that the best way, if one saw a rise, was to cast a foot or two to the side to which the trout seemed to be travelling and then to let the flies lie for a few seconds, not moving them through the water at all. If they floated on the surface like dry flies, so much the better, but at all costs the ripple caused by their rapid movement over the surface must be avoided. This method I have found very effective in calm water both on the loch at home and elsewhere, though it means that one has to strike more quickly than when working a fly in the more usual way.

Sometimes the mist which still lies in drifts and patches in the glen below makes one last effort to rally against the growing power of the sun, and for a few minutes it eddies up from the west end of the loch, hiding the shore and the boat-house. One can no longer see the rises of trout which one hears through the whiteness, and on the heather of the far hillside the cock grouse talk intimately to one another. Then at last the sun breaks finally through the mist sucking up the remnants which linger in the glens and gullies. The grouse move off to the higher ground where bees work. Myriads of flies rise from the drying heather, and all the wild life of the hills settles to the rare enjoyment of a still hot summer's day.

The other picture of the loch which I often see is of the long evenings of June and July. Here, where the slopes of the Ochils look north across the valley to the distant line of the Grampians, we get in summer the very last glow of twilight, and there are a few weeks round midsummer when in clear weather it would be possible with no great effort to read a book all through the night. In the days of early bedtime my room on such nights would seem too light for sleep, as through the open window came the sound of the birds still awake, and the smells of grass and trees and summer. Later, when nursery days had begun to recede, evenings like these were times for walks, sometimes back along the old grass road into the hills when we started off to go only a short distance and were tempted on and on by the soft light and the quiet and the smell of warm grass cooling as the twilight came. But most often we took our rods to the loch to find the wind fallen to a dead calm and trout rising all over the smooth surface, a few feeding quietly but by far the most jumping and splashing as if they, too, were happy on such an evening.

This evening fishing was often fast and exciting, but with the trout rising short one struck wildly, sometimes missing them altogether, sometimes striking them roughly and unexpectedly when the tail fly was often left behind or occasionally hooking them in the side or the tail as they turned away. The absence of the precision and certainty of sight and touch possible

in the day-time makes this fishing in the failing light a sport
by itself, holding its own excitements and thrills, intense and
peculiar. The whole outlook and attitude of mind seem
altered with the change of light. Distances seem greater ;
water which one knows in daylight to be clear and shallow
becomes black and sinister, trees and flowers smell more
intensely, and in the silence sounds have a new and deeper
significance. Blind people, they say, develop the other senses
far beyond their stage of development in those with normal
sight. So at night as sight begins to fail, the other senses
become more receptive and acute.

When the wild abandon of the main evening rise is over,
a few fish may continue feeding more quietly in the growing
darkness, cruising near the surface and sucking dead flies
drifting on the water, and these, though the rises are hard to
see, one has more chance of catching. But after a time even
they become less frequent and finally stop. The loch is quiet
again, but often some time before midnight a ripple spreads
from the west, drifting to the side the moths and midges lying
drowned on the surface. I used to think that it was the
breeze which comes before the dawn, come before its time,
though in fact on these long evenings the dawn was then
not far off. The growing ripple breaks the spell, rousing us
as we drift, to the knowledge that the night is nearly over
and that we are tired. We turn the boat for the shore, guiding
her bows into the boat-house where climbing broom and honey-
suckle almost cover the thatch of the roof, disturbing as we
drift in the pied wagtail which every year nests on the ledge
under the rafters.

Across the stile the path by which we climbed to the
loch earlier in the evening runs through thin grass where the
stone of the hillside has worn almost through the turf. Here
in summer yellow crowsfoot grows and a stretch of thyme,
the patches varying through all the shades from deepest to
palest crimson. Above the path, black against the last of
the sunset, the old Scots firs crown the hill top. To-day the
slopes of the hill are covered with young woods which have
grown up to and around the trunks of the old trees, but when

46

we first made the loch, and for several years after, the hillside was of bare benty turf covered with rabbit holes and patches of scree right to the top. Here the old trees clung as they still cling to their hold, the bark of their trunks roughened and lichen covered, their tops flattened with age and their roots sunk in a soft green carpet of blaeberry plants.

From the hilltop one looks down on the wide stretch of the darkening valley and over to the soft green line of hills. Through the half-light they glow as if with dim reflected sunlight absorbed and stored up through the long summer day. Behind Ben Lomond the last of the sunset has not yet died. Ben Ledi and Ben Vorlich are still sharp against its light, while farther north the outline of the hills behind Crieff and the Sma' Glen seems already to be silhouetted against the growing brightness of sunrise ; and above the black of the old fir branches and out beyond them on all sides stretch vast tracts of silent limitless space.

More than anything in Nature, the night and the stars overwhelm the mind, draining it of coherent thought. From the edge of the hilltop the ground falls steeply, fading from sight into the long gradual slope to the distant shadows of the valley. Only the immensity of the sky and the stars and the night remains, and I, so small beneath them, am glad to put out my hand to feel in the growing dark the rough friendly bark of the old trees standing by my side.

CHAPTER V

TOWN AND COUNTRY

IN re-reading what I have written, I feel that the impression has perhaps been given that we spent all our time in the country. This was unfortunately far from being the case, though there is no doubt that for a number of years we were exceptionally lucky in the amount of time we were able to spend there. Each autumn in the first days of October, Foswell was closed, and the whole household moved back to Edinburgh to be there continuously, except for a short time at Christmas, till Easter of the following year. We dreaded the approach of the date for the return to Edinburgh which seemed like the approach of a dark tunnel through which we must pass to reach the fresh air and sunlight of the spring. As we left Princes Street station and drove to our Edinburgh house through streets where the light of gas lamps reflected on wet pavements, and shrivelled elm leaves drifted from grimy gardens, there seemed little hope left.

And yet the picture which I have in my mind's eye of our nursery in Edinburgh is by no means a cheerless one. A tall guard with a brightly polished rail on top stood in front of the high fireplace, and above the mantelpiece ran a little ledge on which stood a row of miniature animals, dogs and horses and elephants—a Noah's Ark assortment, added to now and then as we acquired new treasures. On the wall above, in black and gold frames, were two Morlands, "The Return from Market" and "The Citizen's Retreat," pictures which worried and puzzled me with their incongruous and unexpected grouping of animals and humans. Besides the Morlands there were four cheerful coloured pictures of stage coaches at full speed, and above the table a cuckoo clock.

In the early years my usual perch was the window seat close to the fireplace from which one could see down the street in both directions, and below which was a big box where all our toys were kept. There was a black Sambo with one eye, a Polar Bear on wheels, rather the worse for wear near the tail and far from clean, and at one end of the box a pile of oblong books containing the varied adventures of a family of Dutch dolls and a gollywog, told in simple verse whose charm was only equalled by the fascination of the pictures. I loved these books, and each year when my birthday came round, a new volume was added until, to my bitter sorrow, the adventures of the versatile gollywogs came to an end.

But of all the contents of the box, what chiefly captured my imagination and fascinated me in the early years was a wooden puzzle, the pieces of which when put together formed a highly coloured picture of Nansen approaching the North Pole. Unluckily a few important pieces, including the Pole itself, were missing, and time and again I would put together those I had, only to be mocked and tantalized to the verge of tears by the half-finished picture of dogs and sledges and green ice against a background of Northern Lights rising in a crescent of brightening colour towards their culminating point above the missing Pole. To find the lost pieces the box in the window seat was ransacked again and again, every cupboard in the house was searched, and even the nursery coal hole was cleared out lest the pieces had somehow been thrown away. But they were never found, nor was it possible to find where the puzzle had been bought or to get it repeated in any of the toy shops, and only slowly and painfully did I at last reconcile myself to the bitter knowledge that the picture would always remain for me incomplete.

Looking back on that time, it seems very clear that we entirely failed to make the best of what was after all a very normal and tolerably happy situation. Instead, we chose to keep our eyes tight shut to the fact that we must spend a large part of the year in Edinburgh, regarding ourselves as only temporary visitors, in town under protest, counting the days till we could leave it. Our feelings in the matter were admirably expressed and perhaps reflected by the conduct of Garry, the little mongrel terrier who had been found wandering half starved in the woods at Foswell and who, gradually over-coming an extreme timidity the outcome of early ill-treatment, became and remained for the nine years of his life with us our devoted and constant companion. Edinburgh was for him a dreary waste from which he looked steadily back to the hills and the rabbits of home, nor during all the winters he spent with us in Edinburgh did he ever reconcile or accustom him-self to town life. I can see him now trotting down the street as if the place belonged to him, or sitting quiet and aloof in the centre of the roadway regardless of traffic, thinking his thoughts. Every now and then as the winter went on, Garry would disappear, and gradually we came to know that on these occasions we would find him at Princes Street station waiting by the platform from which the Perth train leaves, and once when Nurse was packing a suitcase for one of us, Garry, determined not to be left behind, came dragging in his mouth the little brown rug on which he slept.

Other impressions of those winters in Edinburgh come back to the recollection, recalled now by sounds or smells which start in the mind threads of association. As Christmas came near there were many children's parties. For the full enjoyment of these, our predominantly country upbringing and our dislike of town life hardly fitted us, and acceptance of the invitations was often a matter of reluctance ; but when we did go they usually proved to be, like so much else in life, less distasteful in reality than in contemplation, and especially was this the case with the parties about the time of Hallowe'en when ducking for apples was the centre of the entertainment. In late autumn the fruit shops were filled with a variety of apple with vivid red skin and a centre of crisp almost snow-white fruit. Its scent is sweet and distinctive and to-day recalls to me scenes in bright warm nurseries and drawing-rooms where, crowded round baths and tubs in which floated numbers of shining red apples, we tried one after another to pierce them with forks dropped from high chairs, or, if we were older and more venturesome, to duck our heads in the water and grasp the apples in our teeth.

Those were the days when large formal dinner-parties

were the fashion. Each spring my parents gave three such parties, functions which, if they gave little real satisfaction either to hosts or guests, at least provided a full measure of excitement to us children. I well remember the thrill of watching my mother choosing what to me seemed dishes of exquisite rareness and delicacy from the list submitted by the special cook who for such occasions was rather unnecessarily called in to supplement the considerable ability of Annie.

On the night of the party we would hang in speechless excitement over the banisters on the landing outside the nursery door to see the guests arriving, the ladies to disappear into my mother's bedroom where Nurse helped them to remove cloaks and coats, a function which enabled her later to describe to us the details of the more striking dresses. Later, when the last of the party had disappeared into the dining-room, we would creep downstairs to sit on the bottom steps of the staircase and there take heavy toll of the half-finished serving dishes as they were removed after each course, wondering as we did so at the meaningless volume of incoherent sound which came from the dining-room each time the door was opened.

The excitement and bustle of such evenings is associated in my mind with the sound from without of the waltzes of Richard and Johann Strauss and selections from the better-known classical composers played by itinerant bands of German and Austrian musicians who tramped the streets. Clad in dark wine-coloured uniforms and wearing stiff military caps they grouped themselves and their flimsy music-stands beneath street lamps, and while gas-light glittered on instruments of shining brass and silver, cold grey northern streets heard through the night the music of Vienna.

Foswell being shut, there were no week-ends in the country during the autumn, but as time went on an oasis in the waste of winter came in sight, for each Christmas we all went out to Cloan, my uncle's house, for the three weeks' holidays. The world-wide publicity which has transformed the once peaceful Crieff Junction into the modern Gleneagles Station has happily left untouched the near-by station at Auchterarder, and to-day it still retains much of the aspect and character which it had in my childhood. The clipped yew trees where in spring I looked for thrushes' nests are still there, the sparrows still nest on the under side of the wooden foot-bridge regardless of the noise and the smoke from the trains so close below them, and in summer trails of nasturtium still climb the legs of the notice-board which bears the station's name. Stepping down on a winter's evening from the warmth of the carriage on to a platform hard with frost and dimly lit by the yellow light of oil lamps, it seems that little has changed there since the winter nights years ago when we came from town full of excitement at the thought of the holidays and the smell of the country air.

In those short days of winter and living in a house where one was then to some extent a visitor, it was not surprising that among the impressions made on my mind by those Christmas holidays, the details of the house itself had a large place. In the big Red bedroom near the top of the house where we slept was a huge four-poster bed with canopy and side curtains of red repp covered with a pattern of white *fleur de lys*. Lost in its wide expanse, I would lie awake watching the light of the wood fire make flickering patterns on the ceiling, fading and then brightening as a charred stick burst into momentary flame, to die again to a glow and then at last to soft grey ash as I slept. In the schoolroom where we had our meals, the cups and plates had a pattern of twisted green dragons on the thick china, a pattern which at this moment recalls the scene vividly to my mind, and especially a tall narrow strip of a cupboard let into a corner of the wall from which my grandmother's maid, who ruled the schoolroom, produced exciting tins, and a delicious brand of thick biscuit peculiar to the local baker.

Of the grown up people in the house—and to me they seemed *very* grown up—I stood rather in awe. Certainly one felt, and not without reason, that at Cloan one moved in a world where weighty and serious matters were afoot, and I came to look on our big Red bedroom as a kind of island fortress set in a wide strange sea, all the more welcome that to get to it one had to pass fearfully the foot of the twisting stair which led to the hollow-sounding rooms in the tower, or through lengths of passage from whose walls looked down austere German writers and philosophers.

There were, I think, others at Cloan who had their islands, very different from what the Red bedroom was to us, but still islands. On the first floor were the rooms in which my uncle from London spent so much of his time enveloped in an atmosphere of cigar-smoke, red-covered dispatch boxes and high affairs. From them he emerged for the long walks in which all my family indulge, to preside at meals when suddenly, in the midst of talk on serious topics would come kindly cross-examination as to our day's activities, or occasionally to relax in the after-dinner warmth of the drawing-room and tell us ghost stories made more vivid by the wind in the trees outside, and the thought of the dark passages upstairs which we must soon face. The island on which my Oxford uncle lived was very different. It occupied no fixed point in the geography of Cloan but went where he went, a land of thought and contemplation into which he could and did retire at a moment's notice, suddenly absorbed into his own thoughts while sitting at table, while walking outside, or even while standing in the front hall, the carriage or the car waiting to take him to catch a train. His was a remote island, but one where I felt he would always welcome a visitor, though on the rare occasions when I penetrated to it as a child, I found it difficult to know my way about. My aunt's island was different again, a populous place full of ceaseless human activity where she moved with such tireless energy that one felt her intense interest to be not like that of her brothers in the contemplation of ultimate principles of law, science and philosophy, but rather in people, their lives and their thoughts.

But overriding and in a wonderful way uniting all these spheres of thought and activity was the room where my grandmother passed, in bed, the last fourteen of her one hundred years of life. From it she maintained to the very last a wide and lively interest in the outside world. She had in a degree unequalled in the experience of any who knew her the power of projecting herself into the interests and activities of others. No interests were too obscure, too divergent, or too trivial for her understanding and sympathy. I believe that this was given no more readily and freely to those who came to her room to talk of great matters of Religion, State, Science, or Politics, than to us when as children we came to tell her of our walks and our fishing, of the birds and the animals and the wild flowers, while we sat by her nibbling the little coffee-flavoured chocolate beans which she kept for us in the silver-topped box at her bedside.

CHAPTER VI

WINTER AND SPRING

THE burn in the glen below Cloan was in these winter days no longer a centre of interest to me. It ran cold and shrunken and black between snow banks, and sometimes you could only dimly see it moving in long wriggling bubbles of water and air through the white and grey of the ice. There was no hint of trout, and such was the effect of the changed appearance of the place that during these holidays I believe that I thought little more of them than I thought of the summer green of the bare trees. Once only were we reminded vividly that the trout were still there. One year after a period of fresh open weather, it turned suddenly cold, and for three windless nights it froze very hard. The pond by the keeper's house was frozen over with keen clear black ice, and on the third day we could walk on it and see below us the trout moving among the weeds. I suppose this must often happen, but it is a thing which I had never seen before nor have I ever seen it since.

In the winters following the making of the loch in the hills behind Foswell, our chief interest and anxiety came to be whether the frost would come hard enough to let us skate, and each evening we put out on the window-sill of our bedroom at Cloan the lid of a tin of tooth powder filled with water which we hoped to find frozen solid by morning. Each morning when I woke in the big bed I would ask about the weather, and Nurse was hard put to it to pacify me on the many mornings when she had to report that it was raining, or that during the night the frost had gone. But for all that, there were often holidays when we had hard frost, if not at Christmas at least after New Year and before we went back to Edinburgh in the middle of January. Quite often the loch was frozen over hard enough to make skating safe, though usually the wind in that exposed place had made the ice rough and impossible or snow had spoiled the surface. Once at least the fall at Connel's Spout was frozen solid, and the rock was hung with long cones of ice tapering to finest points which we broke off and carried as spears until they melted and broke in our soaked and frozen hands.

The coming of winter seemed to shift the focus and concentration of eye and mind. In summer they were for the hills and the burns, but now the hills, wind-swept and inaccessible, were often hidden by mist and driving snow, while the burns were buried in drifts or still and silent under the ice. Instead, the woods which in summer after the miracle of their first green had passed, one tended to take for granted, acquired a new meaning and significance. Where the leaves had gone, the shapes and outlines of the stems and branches emerged in the full beauty of form and design. Colours, too, acquired a new depth and prominence, and looking over the glen from the hill road behind Foswell you could pick out each variety of tree with a certainty not possible at other times of the year. A yellow tinge in a bank of silver grey marked the European larch from the red brown of the Japanese variety under which the mossy ground was covered with a bright russet carpet of fine needles. The Norway spruce was dark green almost to the borders of black, while the Scots fir and Sitka spruce wore the blue-and-green tartan of the Campbells. Down by the burn, the brown of the alders and birches already had a tinge of purple from the bloom on the young swelling buds, and as one looked over the tree tops a blue puff of smoke would sometimes seem to shoot out from among the oaks to scatter and disintegrate into a little flock of pigeons bound for the corn stacks or the stubbles.

From the Foswell side of the glen you look across far over the tree tops to a bare hillside which stretches up from the edge of the wood to the farm road opposite. In summer this hillside is covered with bents and patches of bracken, but when winter comes the bents die down, the brackens wither and dwindle to almost nothing, and the hillside is worn and eaten threadbare. Then the moss covering the poor soil beneath the grass comes into its own, and unless the snow is on it, the whole slope becomes vivid with emerald green velvet over which the tips of the mossy tendrils spread a yellow silky sheen.

Looking across the glen in these winter holidays, you would almost think that the spring grass had come before its time, but the white and brown patches on the nibbled roots and lower branches of the surrounding trees showed that the green held no nourishment even for the starving rabbits. When the snow lay deep on the hills and the frozen ground was too hard for worms and insects, the woods became more than ever a centre of the life of the animals. Under the thick cover of the spruces and Douglas firs the ground remained black and soft in all but the hardest weather, and here the birds congregated, while from the burrows on the open slopes outside the woods, all the rabbit runs led to the shelter of the trees. Round the burrows, shreds and tufts of moss lay in the snow where the rabbits had scraped through looking for food, and at the edges of the holes the traffic of rabbits' feet had worn the snow into thin transparent coatings of crystal and silver through which showed the green of the moss below. In those days, my favourite books were Thomson-Seton's animal stories and especially Long's *Northern Trails* with its fascinating sketches of animals. The woods at Cloan held nothing more exciting than rabbits and hares and an occasional fox, but with Long's pictures before my eyes it needed little imagination to magnify the tracks in the snow of Perthshire into those of wolf and mink and snow leopard from the farthest and wildest parts of North America.

Not all the animals came to the shelter of the woods, but those which stayed out on the open hills during the winter were often hard put to it to struggle through to the spring. The tops of many of the high ridges in the Ochils are covered with stretches of peat hag, and here the mountain hares, blue in summer but now white in their winter coats, had congregated for such shelter as they could find. Deep cuttings run twisting and maze-like through the peat leaving between them curiously shaped islands and peninsulas like a bas-relief map of some of the more grotesque geological formations of the earth's surface. At the edge of each peninsula and island, masses of peat and heather overhang the cutting below like some slow-moving liquid dropping from above, forming as they hang suspended, little holes and tunnels where the hares shelter. The Providence which cares for animals in winter alone knows what they find to eat, or how they live to see the spring. Many, I am afraid, do not.

Often during hard winters these high slopes of the hills showed evidence that it was not only the rabbits and the hares that found the struggle for existence a hard one. One day, not far from home, I was climbing a high ridge. There was snow on the ground through which showed the tops of the longer grasses, but it was hard and crusted with the strong wind, and the sun glittered on its icy surface. Near the crest of the

ridge, I came to a part of the hill covered with a tall thick rush-like grass whose stalk ends in a cluster of dark brown seeds. The stalks showed above the snow, the heads drooping with the weight of the seeds to hang a few inches above its surface. As I came nearer I became aware of faint chirpings and of little quick movements among the stalks, and then I saw that in and out among the hanging seed heads hurried a flock of snow buntings. As I watched, I saw that each bird would stretch up to reach the seed on an overhanging stalk before hurrying on to the next as if engaged on an urgent and vital task ; and on that cold hillside so indeed they were. So engrossed in their feeding were they that even when I came quite near they only fluttered on a few yards and started feeding again.

Wild and bitter winter weather seems often to induce in

us when we are indoors a strange sense of security and cosiness.
It comes, I think, from more than the mere contrast between
lamp-lit rooms and warm beds and the cold of the outside
world, and I have sometimes wondered whether there is not
in us a lingering remnant of that instinct which makes certain
animals on the approach of winter retire into holes in
the ground and hollow trees, into beds of dead leaves or deep
nests in the dry withered grass. Lying at night in the great
four-poster at Cloan, I would in fancy build for myself a
warm house in the woods. Searching out a tree whose lower
branches drooped to the ground, I would add to and rein-
force the canopy spread by Nature over the space within ; I
would fill all the little chinks and holes in the walls with leaves
and grass till none remained and the wind howled against
my house powerless to blow through it, while snow falling on
the roof muffled and hid my hiding-place as I lay inside cosy
and secure. My house was seldom complete before I fell asleep,
sharing a warm oblivion with the animals which sleep through
the winter weather.

Looking down to the valley, the same prominence of shape
and outline which marked the woods and fields of the nearer
landscape met the eye, though here, save in the evening, the
colours were more subdued, dark browns and purples of
ploughed fields and distant woods contrasting with black and
white of snow and rock on the far hills. Over the wide brown
stretch of the heathery woodland behind Strathallan a smudge
of blue smoke showed where the foresters were burning brush-
wood, and farther west a bank of cloud would come boiling and
eddying up to the head waters of the Allan where the weather of
east and west so often meet. Directly below us was the misty
grey-brown of the bare oak woods at Kincardine. The wide
pool of sombre colouring was broken at intervals by sudden
dark spires which shot up far above the surrounding wood
marking where the tall old spruce trees towered, their long
drooping branches forming round the central stem a series of
green tents of foliage inside which the squirrels slept, while
wrens and tits and other small wood birds found warmth
and shelter through the winter months.

On the Grampians opposite, the amount of snow varied season by season. Sometimes the hills were only mottled black and white though usually Ben Vorlich had a coat of unbroken white, while in the deep corrie on the side of Ben-a-Chonzie which overlooks Crieff a drift lay crescent-shaped each winter and often on till early June. More often the hills were pure white, and on fine winter evenings the changing colours on the snow-fields were almost beyond belief. By early afternoon, a touch of lemon gold would creep into the brilliance of the sunlight, the gold brightened and deepened, changing as one watched to pink, and then to red, which in its turn faded until only the tops of the highest hills caught the last of the light. To the east the sky had changed to grey and then to dark-blue, and as the colour deepened it threw into relief the white cone of Mount Blair and the snow on the high shoulders of the hills of Angus.

About the middle of January we all went back to Edinburgh to face the long term which lay between us and Easter. I always felt this the deadest period of the whole year in town, and had to resort to all sorts of devices and fancies to console myself. I remembered that February was the shortest month of the year, that this term had, perhaps, one day less than last, that the days were lengthening and that even now men were fishing on the Tay. Salmon fishing in those days meant so little to me that I hardly felt that it counted, but there was always some thrill to be got from the knowledge, and the sight of fresh salmon in the shops was exciting. Gradually the dead season wore through, and as the beginning of March and the start of trout fishing came round, we climbed from the shadows.

It was about this time I used to undergo that experience which each spring strikes me anew as one of the strangest of the many wonderful powers of memory. I mean the sudden transformation by which in a single flash the focus of mental vision shifts from the things of winter to those of spring. The experience is too common to all of us to need description, nor is it capable of adequate description and still less of analysis. It comes to us unexpected and unheralded, often at incongruous times and in strange places, and in a moment of surging exultation the scenes and scents of spring already complete in every detail are with us again. But wonderful as is this unexpected but unfailing transformation, it cannot compare with other miracles constantly happening in the world of Nature. To the migratory fish in the sea comes suddenly the memory of fresh water, the urge to return, and the power to select from a hundred rivers that where it was hatched, and some similar influence of memory or instinct launches each year on their long journeys thousands of our spring birds.

I used to find that as the opening of the fishing season came nearer, my anticipation and longing became focused on one burn, or even on one pool. I remembered a trout seen or lost in it the previous season. The conviction grew that this time by the use of some new manœuvre or method of approach I would catch it, and I longed to be there. At night, before I fell asleep, I would construct elaborate and wholly fanciful days on one of the burns, days in which everything down to the smallest detail was thought out and complete, the picture of the place vivid before me. In planning and devising these imaginary days, I took special pleasure in the preliminary detail and seldom had the expedition passed the preparatory stages before I had fallen asleep. This was perhaps as well, for all but a supremely successful day would have seemed an anticlimax after the high degree of anticipation with which in my fancy it had been prepared.

Occasionally we went to the country for a week-end near the beginning of March, but in any event the end of the month saw us back there again, and the flimsy castles in the air which I had constructed during the past six weeks had then to withstand the chilling blasts of cold reality. Spring is apt to come late on these north-facing slopes of the Ochils, and there may be long periods when dry east winds tear in from the coast and the temperature hovers about freezing-point. There are some seasons when the worst snowstorm of the year comes well on in March, or even in April when the ewes lamb, and many when the hollows on the hillsides and by the burns hold far into April the hard residue of deep drifts coated with the dry seeds of heather and rush, fragments of stick and grass and all the accumulation of wind-swept days, while trickles of icy water seep over brown and flattened rushes into the burn below.

There is a glittering brilliance about the days of mid-April in the north which you get at no other time of year. The melting of the snow has completed the process by which Nature clears from the land the last signs of the litter and decay of winter, and the air, washed clean by constant rain, has a freshness proper to the morning of the year. At no other season, save perhaps when the first sharp frosts come in October, does one get such a clearness of atmosphere and distance of view, and for walking in our hills April days have no equal. I believe, too, that as the year goes on and the scents and colours of summer multiply, the senses get a little dulled either because their power of absorption approaches saturation, or more likely because our minds get lazy, taking for granted the wealth of beauty on all sides and so missing some of its finer and more subtle shades. But in April the senses are fresh and keen and receptive. The bleached silver whiteness of the bents seems never so vivid nor their clean astringent scent so strong. In the glens the gleaming threads of the burns show more clearly than in summer, for now they run brimful from springs filled by the melting snow, and are not yet hidden among the grass and rushes which mask them in the summer.

Among the trees of our own glen where the pools in the burn get some shelter from the wind, and the water has lost the bitter coldness of the newly melting snow-drifts, you can get a few trout in early April. I do not think the brown trout of the burn ever really stops feeding during the winter unless sometimes from sheer lack of things to eat, nor does he lose condition like the trout of the loch or the larger low-ground streams, probably because he does not depend so much on surface feeding. But as you get up near the source of the burn, the coldness of the water makes him lazy and less inclined for food, and here you will get little. Often in April I would see the burns running full and very tempting, the pools and streams at a level which six weeks later would make me certain of a big basket ; but in the gullies and hollows the grass lay matted and flattened, exposing the summer runways and tunnels of the field mice which still lay snug in the dry heart of the dead bents, and showing that the snow was only newly off the hill. On such a day, despite the tempting height of the burn, I would catch few trout, while in the April sunshine I would see through the clear water of the pools faint cloud shadows thrown by the eddies on the gravel below and the reflections of the ripples like wide-meshed nets of pale golden light, the whole in constant change and motion.

But if the spring lingered during these April days and the east wind still blew from the North Sea keeping the trees bare and parching the first shoots of young grass round the hill springs, there were other signs which showed that winter was passing. Each day the plover moved farther and farther up the hill from the low ground where they had wintered, and before long were crying and tumbling and swooping over their old nesting grounds among the bents and rushes, and on the stubbles their first tentative scrapes began to appear. The curlew followed, and soon all through the hills you would see them soaring and gliding, trying again their spring call, half forgotten after months of silence. In the rushes at the head of a burn I would disturb mallard choosing a nesting-place, and each season a pair of golden plover appeared in almost exactly the same part of the hill. Over on the Grampians smudges of smoke showed where the keepers were hurrying to get the old heather burned before the burning season ended, and from our own hills, too, came the smell of grass fires as the shepherds burned the bents far up on the high shoulders.

CHAPTER VII

GLENDEVON

IF you follow the old peat road which climbs the hill behind Foswell up the steep face of heather ground where stagshorn moss trails through the grass of the path, and across the long shoulder of bents, you come finally to a drystone dyke which marks the beginning of the flatter ground at the top of the ridge.

It often happens that the old dykes in the Ochils form natural dividing lines between sheep grazings of quite different character, on one side bents and on the other heather, a division dating, I suppose, from the days when each small piece of the hillside was separately owned, and perhaps differently grazed, by the farms on the lower slopes. Now, many of the small holdings have been brought together into a single ownership, and the stone dykes, no longer required, are tumbling down and serve no other purpose than as shelter for the sheep and the hares in bad storms, or as a home for the weasels of which the hills have too many ; but the sudden change in the nature of the grazing as you cross the dykes in many cases still persists. So as you come out on to the ridge above Foswell you pass from white bents on to ground dark with old stunted heather, with blaeberry and with cranberry. There are soft peaty parts, too, where the water lies in wet weather and where the sphagnum moss grows in great dome-shaped cushions of pink and green which serve as perches for the curlew and the cock grouse. Looking back from the ridge, it seems that half Scotland lies before you from the Sidlaws and the Carse of Gowrie in the east to Ben Lomond and the hills of Dumbartonshire in the west, the whole picture enclosed and framed within the great wall of the Grampians. The high peaks of Ben Vrackie and Ben-y-gloe, Ben Lawers and the Cobbler peep over the nearer ridges.

The view to the south is in marked contrast. Here you

look into the Ochils themselves, to miles of bents and rushes
with small heather patches, to fold upon fold of quiet rounded
hills rising gradually till they reach their highest point where,
a few miles to the south-west, Ben Cleuch stands at the head
of Glendevon. From where you stand on the ridge, the
bottom of each little valley in the hills is hidden by a nearer
shoulder, nor are the burns at almost any point visible ; but
the fall of the ground and the slope of the glens show to the
imagination what is hidden from the eye, how each small
spring bubbling up under the moss among the rushes trickles
down the hillside to be joined by neighbouring trickles from
near-by springs, the united stream going on to make its contribution to the growing burn in the glen, and it in turn
falling at length into the main stream of the River Devon
which runs in the great fold of the hills to the south.

An expedition to fish the head waters of the Devon was
for us, at the time of which I write, not one to be undertaken
without considerable preparation. The distance from our
house across the hill and down to the Devon valley is little
more than four miles, but to this had to be added at least
another four miles as we fished upstream into the hills where
the best fishing was, and then the eight miles home, so that
the whole distance was one which at that time was rather
beyond my strength. But it sometimes happened that some
errand took the wagonette round to Glendevon or occasionally
McEwan could be spared from the garden for the three hours
which it took for him to drive there and back. The main
drawback to this difficulty of transport was that plans had to
be made some days ahead, and it was a matter of pure chance
whether or not the burns were in good order for fishing on
the chosen day. From the day the expedition was planned,
an added urgency was attached to my nightly petitions that
rain might be sent, though these remained unofficial and
qualified in view of the claims of the farmers whose need for
dry weather for hay or harvest came, I was told, before all
else. Even if no rain fell, there was the excitement of
fishing in comparatively unknown water in a stream which
even in dry weather was bigger than any of the burns I knew

nearer home—and had not my brother and Speed once, when the burns were in spate, brought home from the Devon a basket of over one hundred trout ?

To get by road from our house through the hills to Glendevon, one had to take the side road which follows close along their north face as far as Gleneagles, where the main road to Queensferry runs through the Ochils. Major, the black cob, well accustomed to the steep hills on the roads round Foswell, was no believer in starting out at a pace faster than that which he proposed to maintain, and this was slow enough ; nor did McEwan hurry him. Especially if the burns were in good order, we grudged each moment of the drive, but in fact it would have been hard to find a road where one could more pleasantly spend an hour on a summer morning sitting behind the jog-trot of a leisurely horse.

To the south of the road the ground rose gradually from arable to grass land, and then to rough pasture with patches of whin ending in a drystone dyke beyond which was the heather and bents of the hillside. From so close in under the face of the hill you could trace every little hollow and gully and each well-known detail. You could see the scattered larches standing at the foot of the heather, stunted and weather-beaten, the turf round their roots beaten hard and bare by sheep pressing for shelter round trunks polished with their rubbing. You could look up into the steep glen of Cornhill where the blaeberry and heather of the hills look steeply down on the green of the burn side. Where it leaves the heather, the burn falls under a water-gate into an oak wood and presently the road crosses it on a narrow stone bridge at an awkward bend, the stream on the low side overhung with a tangle of bird cherry as it runs on to join a larger burn in the glen below.

Every season makes that road lovely. In May, the banks and ditches are clothed in the rich new green of dog mercury among which the young rabbits move, the drooping branches of the larch trees are bright with little plumes of red, and the beeches wear the delicate green whose matchless beauty is

66

shown to us in its full glory only for a few days each spring. Later, the wild geranium covers in mauve and purple the bank beside one stretch of the road, and then comes the pink and white of the wild rose.   Below the road, a field's breadth away, is a low grey dyke and across it as we pass the rabbits and the cock pheasants which have been feeding in the roadside field disappear into the thickness of the Kincardine woods. Down there in the glen, hidden by the trees over which the pigeons circle, runs a burn fed by the strong springs in Gleneagles, the farthest of them rising on the hill only a little distance from the Devon to which we are going.

Often when fishing and walking in the hills at home, I have wondered what that country was like long ago.   It would be fascinating to see it as it was when the old black timbers which here and there one finds sunk in the peat were growing trees ; to know if plover and curlew called then in the glens ; whether grass of parnassus and mimulus grew by the burnside where they grow to-day ; whether the creamy foam of meadowsweet filled the meadows and fringed the streams as it does now ; to know, too, whether the small black trout far up at the head of the burns are the descendants of fish which lived in these same pools centuries ago.   History confines itself to recording more important if less interesting things, so we shall never know the full story of the burns, but we do know that the burn in the glen below the road where the pigeons circle was fished by the Marquis of Montrose, who as a boy lived at the old Castle of Kincardine, and that in 1628 when he was lying ill at St. Andrews, trout from it were sent to tempt the appetite of convalescence.

On the main road which climbs through Gleneagles, Major's trot becomes gradually slower, till after passing the old toll house, it falls to a walk.   Here the road passes under a steep hill face covered with patches of fern growing among banks of scree.   Across these the sheep move in single file on their little paths, sending small stones rolling and jumping down the slope and sometimes starting avalanches of stones to the peril of the passer-by and the despair of the road authorities.   Above the scree a great wall of rock overhangs the slope and out from its face circle and tumble the jackdaws which live in its holes and niches. The head of the glen comes suddenly ; Major quickens his pace as the slope eases off, and beyond an old spruce strip where hoodie crows nest, the ground starts to fall to the valley of the Devon.

The part of the upper Devon valley which we most often fished might have been planned by Nature with an eye to the needs of a trout fisher. A short way upstream from the point where we leave McEwan and the wagonette, a good-sized stream falls into the Devon on the south side. In the angle where the two streams meet, a steep meadow slopes up to a shepherd's cottage backed by Scots firs, a meadow which in June and July is a mass of wild flowers, among them the same St. Baldred's Money which grows at Coulshill. Our usual plan was to fish up the side stream, first with fly and then when it grew too small, with worm, to the very source of the burn, following as far as the trout could go each of the branches into which the burn splits near its top. Then we would cross a high ridge and come down on a more distant burn which flowed northwards at right angles to join the Devon at the lonely shepherd's cottage at Backhill. This we would follow, finally fishing our way back down the main stream to our starting-point, having completed a circuit of more than five miles, fishing nearly the whole way.

There were few burns more pleasant to fish than that up which we started from the Devon. Where it skirted the foot of the meadow was a series of deep little waterfall pools full of trout, but they called for accurate casting, particularly at the tail of each where the rocky sides closed in, narrowing the pool to a mere foot or two across. The boulders whose tops rose above the surface of the pools and the rock at the lip of each successive fall were covered with cushions of moss, and mimulus both yellow and mottled grew in the sand and gravel beside the water. Rock faces covered with damp mosses and fringed at the top with overhanging thyme and harebells rose above some of the deeper pools, and from beneath these as one came upstream, a water ousel would often fly out to perch on a stone a few yards above, scolding and bobbing in indignation.

There is not much heather on this part of the hill, and after crossing a dyke which divided the meadow ground from the hill, one came out into an open glen, bents and bracken on either slope, and little streams running down rush-filled gullies on each side to join the main burn. As we followed the burn, the glen grew narrower and the hills steeper. The turns and bends of the stream hid the larger glen from which we had climbed, and but for an occasional glimpse of woods far down Glendevon there was nothing to be seen but bents and rushes and water, and sheep moving on the hillside.

Often as summer went on and the lambs grew strong and independent, we would come on them sleeping under patches of rushes or bracken near the burn side, the ewes having left them to their own devices while they moved up the hillside in search of sweeter grazing. Sometimes moving quietly, I have come right up to them and have been able to put my hand on them where they lay. Some when wakened would dash off in alarm, others after going a few steps would stop and stretch black legs, their tails wriggling in an ecstasy of luxurious sleepiness, showing more curiosity than alarm. One woke to the conviction that I was his mother, coming to me and following me closely for some little way, and a very young one I remember which, despite the frenzied protests of the ewe, ran to a large grey boulder near by and was only with difficulty persuaded that neither milk nor protection was to be obtained from it.

The top of the burn approaches the 2,000 feet contour, and as one came near it one sometimes reached the lower level of the mist which often lies along the top of the Ochils. As one neared its edge, there came a feeling of the imminence of some great thing hanging above. The sound of burn water falling in the distance became dulled and subdued, then a cold movement of air stirred on one's face, tiny particles of moisture appeared on the surface of tweeds and stockings, and in a few yards one was surrounded by the mist.

When fishing alone, I was never very good at pushing into thick mist unless fishing a burn which I knew very well. All around had suddenly become unfamiliar and alarming. The

70

slope of the hillside seemed steeper, and where it disappeared into the greyness above, it seemed to rise up not to the rounded shoulders of bents which I knew but to some great height foreign and unknown to these hills. Dark shapes of great size moved on the hill above, and even the discovery that these were only ewes, their fleeces damp and glistening with the mist's dewdrops, failed to dispel altogether a feeling of vague alarm.

Foolish as much of this was, there was in fact an appreciable risk of getting lost in these hills so similar in shape and outline. Once I had set off to climb Ben Cleuch at the head of the Devon. Mist came down before I reached the top, but this time I went on and reaching the cairn sat to eat my lunch in a cold thick greyness. Then I set off down the slope for home. When I emerged from the mist 200 feet lower, it seemed that the valley which stretched below me was nearer than I had remembered it to be, the river winding through it seemed bigger and broader than either the Allan or the Earn; but such is the power of the imagination to persuade the eye that it sees in fact what it expects to see, that only slowly did I realize that I had come down on the south side of the hills and was looking over the valley of the Forth.

Near the crest of the ridge which overlooks the farther burn down which we now fished to rejoin the Devon, we climbed through a stretch of peat hags. These were full of blue hares, and as we came round the bends and corners of the deep miniature valleys which weather and water have gradually worn in the peat, we would see them dodging ahead or sometimes would come on them crouching in the holes or under the shelter of the peat banks. On the very top of the ridge were pools of shallow peaty water looking all the blacker for the rich green of the grass round their edges. Mallard often rose from these pools, and occasionally teal, or feathers sailing on the ripples at the water's edge told of their recent visits.

By the time we have fished our way down the main stream of the Devon to our starting-point by the meadow, it is late afternoon. Major, long since back in his stable at home, drowses over his hay, and McEwan locking his rakes and spades in the tool shed, goes home to his tea beside the kitchen fire, while in a wickerwork cage above the window his little ring-dove keeps up an endless cooing. Four miles of hill lie between us and home, with a climb of nearly 1,000 feet before we cross the ridge. If we are pressed for time and have to take the shortest route it means a long climb up the slopes behind the farm house at Glenhead and across the boggy flat beyond. But if we have time to spare and are not too tired, we follow down the Devon for half a mile to where a burn comes in on its north side, fishing up it till our watches tell us it is time to stop. Then we take down our rods, perhaps sitting for a few minutes on the slope above the burn to make a final count of our trout, searching our pockets for any remaining scraps of lunch. It is unwise to sit for long when you are very wet and tired. Feet sodden with burn water remain, while you keep moving, warm and comfortable in boots where hard places have been worn soft by hours of walking. But if you sit for long, boots and feet harden and stiffen, and when you start walking again, for the first time you realize all the miles behind you.

On the south side of the ridge, just before you reach the march dyke which runs along the top, is a slope of bents ankle deep and more. After a day of showers or mist on the hill, the grass is hanging with moisture which soon soaks again our already sodden boots, a refreshing bath of cold water for our tired feet. On this last slope up to the ridge there are few landmarks. On either side and ahead of us the white shoulders of bent-covered hills stretch into the distance, perhaps disappearing into the gathering mist of evening. Behind is the glen of the burn up which we have come, a bend far down it hiding the valley of the Devon with the road and the woods and the signs of habitation. In the days when I fished the burns with Pat, this isolation meant little to me, though often I had no idea where we had come to. But later when I first fished alone, that last half mile over the top of the hills was something of a venture, and as I crossed the march dyke and saw below me the steep familiar glen of the Cornhill burn

72

falling in the distance to the trees of Kincardine, I felt like some bold navigator who, by skilful reckoning through strange seas, has made a happy landfall.

On the path which leads down off the hill, the steep slope tells on tired legs and knees. The sight and the sound of burn water all through a long day have their effect in the evening, and often I have come down the old road from Coulshill or down the path from the high hill walking almost in a dream. The return to the light and warmth of the house calls for a real effort of readjustment, and after a day in the hills eyes and senses are dazed by the sudden change. This is the measure of the remoteness, not in time and space only, of the little world in which we have moved, and in this, I think, lies the secret of the quiet content with which we look back.

In the kitchen at Foswell a great ashet is fetched, and on this a mound of shiny black red-spotted trout is heaped from our baskets. A final count is made, while Annie, perhaps in the middle of preparing dinner, expresses admiration and enthusiasm, concealing the dismay with which the prospect of the subsequent disposal of the catch must so often have filled her. Then we climb again the steep stairs to supper in the warmth and the lamplight of the nursery ; and soon to bed, while the soft twilight of the summer night falls on the hills and the burns.

CHAPTER VIII

THE WATER OF MAY

IN late July or early August come the rains which the country people of the north know as the Lammas floods. The farmers await their coming with some anxiety, for should they come before their time they may ruin a late hay crop, while if they come late or linger beyond their time, heavy fields of ripening corn may be laid so flat that mechanical reapers cannot cut them. Then the lying crop must be cut slowly and laboriously with scythes, each sheaf gathered and tied by hand with bands made of twisted lengths of straw.

For the fisherman, too, these rains are important, for they come at a time when in many parts of the country the big sea-trout are waiting in estuaries or at river mouths to push their way up to the streams of the upper waters. For us, fishing the burns at Foswell, the rains were opportune, for they usually came just after the end of the school term when the hardly restrained impatience to be once again beside the burns was at last free to satisfy itself in an orgy of fishing.

Of all the burns of which during the months in town I had thought with longing and anticipation, there was one which, as time went on, recurred with increasing frequence to my mind. The Water of May was the farthest away and by far the best of all the burns we fished from Foswell. To fish it entailed an expedition of some importance and one which could hardly be wasted on a day when the burns were not in good order, and so it was that the day chosen for the expedition was often at the time of the Lammas floods.

The burns in the Ochils are apt to empty themselves quickly after rain has stopped, and may in a few hours be again back at a low level, the magic moment for large baskets past till the next flood. So it was always a matter of great concern to us whether or not rain had fallen immediately preceding an expedition, especially one so important as that to the

May, and on the morning chosen I would wake early to find
out what, if any, rain had fallen during the night. McEwan
shared with most gardeners whom I have known the faculty
of describing in great detail the weather during the course of
the night. He would tell you that rain had started at 2 a.m.
continuing till 4.30, with showers thereafter till daybreak,
statements made with such confidence that one could only
assume that he had spent a sleepless night watching the
weather. Sometimes if his report were not favourable I would
feel inclined to question its accuracy, but when he reported
heavy rain I readily accepted it as correct.

Like most of our fishing expeditions, that to the May
entails the use of both fly and worm. The fly casts have been
tied and soaked overnight, but often the worms have to be
collected in the morning. With the ground damp from the
night's rain, we could get any number of the ordinary pink
kind in the garden, but this expedition is a rather special one,
calling for a particularly succulent kind of worm which we
call, quite inaccurately, " Bramble worms," and which live in
the depths of certain heaps of leaf-mould or farmyard manure
of some maturity known to us. By the time the worms are
dug and our rods, flies, and casts collected, Annie has our
lunch ready, and we start out telling the family to expect us
when they see us.

The way over the hills to the valley of the May leads up
the glen past Coulshill. Beside the road the ditches are choked
with wet swathes of bent grass and meadowsweet, and from
the bank overlooking them heads of tall grasses glistening with
rain water hang over and lightly veil a pale blue scatter of
drooping harebells. Below the road the rushes in the meadows
beside the Coulshill burn are beaten down by the rain in
patches of pale green, on the flattened surface of which lie
countless tiny drops of moisture like a sprinkling of silver dust.
The Coulshill burn is full and brown, and the pools under the
trees near the steading are very tempting ; but we have a long
way ahead of us and they must wait till evening when on the
way back there may be time to try them.

Opposite the road which leads to the Cadger's Yett and

looking across the burn to it, a second grassy road leads over the shoulder of the hill, but this one, instead of bearing west to where the watershed overlooks Glendevon, turns slightly to the east and follows the Coulshill burn to the point where it is little more than a trickle lost among thick rushes at the very head of the glen. At an old sheep bridge of wood and turf we cross the burn, and making our way up through wet bracken, join this grassy track on the hillside. In the centre of the path stand little pools of rain-water, and, wet as we now are from the brackens, we splash through them, not sorry to feel on our feet the cold water which must in any event soon soak them. The path runs through stretches of bents, smelling clean and fresh as they dry in the growing breeze. From the bigger tufts where they have sheltered from the rain, little pipits spring into sudden but aimless flight, and all around us as we pass numbers of small silver-grey moths rise from the grass.

Soon the path bends still more to the east, a shoulder of bents shuts off the view down the Coulshill glen to the distant Grampians across whose face drift little rags of white mist, and in a short distance we reach the boundary fence of the farm. Crossing here, and walking on a little way, we find ourselves in a narrow pass with slopes of short bare grass rising steeply on either side. The sheep have made little paths along the face of these slopes, and looking up as you pass you will see them walking in single file far above you. Rabbits sit by their burrows on the hillside, and stonechats rising from the little beds of scree fly off with a flirt of white underwing to sit scolding on near-by boulders. Though there is no record of it, I feel sure that this narrow glen must in days gone by have seen ambushes and fierce fighting, perhaps between the Picts who lived in that country and the Romans who are said to have had an outpost far downstream below Coulshill, looking across to their great camp at Ardoch in Strathallan.

At the top of the pass there is a bog, and in a wet season there is also a tiny pond. From it a burn runs down to the east, but it goes underground at first, though sometimes you can hear it running beneath you as you walk through the pass.

The ground falls gradually down the glen and then more steeply, and the grass in the hollow grows richer and greener. Then just as the pass opens out at its far end, the underground stream from the pond on the watershed comes to the surface, bubbling up into a small pool surrounded by mossy stones below which a little stream, the Water of May, starts off eastwards on its twelve-mile course to join the Earn far down at Forteviot.

Within a very few yards of the point where it emerges from its underground course, the little stream is joined by other trickles coming from the surrounding bog, and it is not long before it has become big enough to hold trout. The easiest plan is to start from this point and fish down, using worm in the little pools of the burn as it runs through the meadow where the shepherd from the near-by cottage cuts his meadow hay and rushes for thatch. But this plan is apt to land one towards evening far down the glen, tired and short of time. The wiser way is to walk on a few miles down the glen and fish back up to the pass. Then after crossing the watershed there may be time to fish the best parts of the Coulshill burn on the way home, and this plan, curbing our impatience to start fishing, we usually adopted.

A little way below the meadow where it first appears, the May enters a deep gully. From its sides black rocky outcrops, which in the higher parts of the Ochils are seldom far from the surface, break in places through the green and look down on the burn, the steep rocks hung with trails of thyme and damp mosses and supporting here and there a tattered rowan tree. Above the gully the hills on either side of the glen rise more gradually, thick round clumps of bracken on the lower slopes (marked on the old maps as the " Ferny Braes ") and then bents and open hill pasture above.

We keep to the south side of the glen along the hillside high above the burn. Through the bents run sheep paths, crossing, dividing and sub-dividing, and lending themselves to the game of railways which I play to myself as we hurry down the glen. At intervals we cross old fences running up the hillside. Some are broken down by the snows of many

77

winters, but a few are still in some sort of repair and here
the tracks converge towards the gaps and gateways, clover
and pink and white yarrow growing in the close turf which
covers soil made firm and rich by the constant trafficking of
sheep.

Here and there on both sides of the valley belts of old timber
run far up the hillside. Some of these belts are now marked
only by ragged lines of scattered trees, the sole survivors of
many gales and the homes of marauding hoodie crows and
sparrow-hawks, but in places time has dealt more kindly.
A mile down from the head of the burn the sheep path which
we have been following cuts through the upper end of one such
belt of Scots firs. Lower down in the same wood the trees are
tall and well grown, but the top reaches the 1,000 feet contour,
and here where we cross they show all the marks of their
altitude and their age. A few still stand erect, their struggle
for existence shown only by their stunted growth and twisted
stems. Some stand dead and rotten, while others, still living,
sway as their loosened roots rise and fall with the wind, waiting
only for the next gale to lay them to join the many whose
rotting limbs and branches lie choked and half buried in rank
grass.

Beyond the wood the track leads gradually downhill
through richer pasture to where two great ash trees stand
beside the ruins of a little farm steading now overgrown with
nettles. The hills round these top waters of the May look
down on little meadows and grassy uplands dotted and scarred
with the marks of a chapter of Ochil history now almost closed.
On both sides of the stream in the flat ground formed by its
bends, and on the shoulders of the surrounding hills, stand the
remains of cottages and farm steadings now deserted. Some
are buildings of no great age, but many are of old drystone
construction dating back more than a century to a time when
the great ash trees which now overhang the ruins must have
been no more than small seedlings, and some are older still.
Beside the ruins can be seen the outlines of old stackyards and
gardens enclosed by turf dykes now little more than grassy
mounds and banks where wild flowers grow and sheep lie

sleeping, while surrounding the steadings and stretching often far up the hillside are the clear outlines of fields once cultivated.

The very names of these old homes are disappearing from the maps, but those that remain speak of the places they marked, quiet remote hill farms where Ochil farmers grew oats and flax in fields long since reverted to the rough grass of the hill, herded black cattle and eked out their livelihood by spinning and weaving the wool of the few black-faced sheep which they kept. Knowehead, Greenhill and Broadheadfold, Littlerig, Lategreen and Rashiehill—the names seem so expressive that did I not know that green and quiet glen, I think they alone would tell me of it.

Now we are far down the glen half-way and more to the little cluster of houses at Pathstruie. The woods which lie beyond are now in sight, but they are unfamiliar and between lie several miles of strange hillside, little green glens and old deserted farms. Alone, I could never, for all my love of the glen, face without an effort these long silent stretches, and I turn now and then for courage to see far back the friendly line of telegraph poles striding in single file up the hill road to Greenhill as they make for the Blaeberry Toll on the watershed from which they will look down to the old roofs of Dunning and out over Strathearn. But to-day, with my brother leading the expedition, with the burn in good fishing order and with the sun shining through clear air washed with the rain and glistening on wet grass and bracken, the distances of the glen have no terrors. Presently, with a mind to the time which it will take us to fish our way home, we slant down to the waterside and put up our rods. Then we turn upstream, five miles of glen and water and grassy hills between us and the narrow pass leading back through the hills to Coulshill Glen, where evening will find us wet and a little footsore, but cheered by the weight on our shoulders and, more and more, by the growing thought of home.

At the point to which we have come, the May, swelled by many little burns and springs, has reached the stage where for the first time it shows signs that soon it will justify the title of " Water " given to it on the maps, somewhere between a large burn and a very little river, but still, I like to think, well on the sunny side of the dividing line. Perhaps its size is best described by the *Old Statistical Account* for Perthshire which refers to it as a " rivulet " full of " very fine-flavoured trout about the size of an herring."

Nearly all the burns run north and south down the face of the Ochils, so that their course is a short one. But a few, notably the Devon and the May, run for part of the way from west to east along the hills and so have a relatively long life before they enter the rivers towards which they flow. It is, I think, for this reason that the May assumes for a few miles in its middle reaches a character and appearance rather different from the small north-flowing burns near home with which we are so familiar. Here are fewer little waterfalls or deep pools. Instead there are broader shallow stretches where the stream flows gently over gravelly beds, the only depth of water close in under the bank. Here and there for no apparent reason the stream takes a sudden bend and flows close in under a high bank where turf and soil have slipped down leaving a bare clay face. The water washes against the foot of the slope and in wet weather when the stream flows strongly, clay and soil are constantly washed down, colouring the water below to the deception of the trout, but sometimes to the benefit of the fisher.

There are places, too, where outcrops of rock jut out at a

bend of the stream. The water meets the outcrop almost at right angles and is deflected in a deep and narrow stream close in under the rock face from whose chinks and ledges wild flowers and grasses overhang the water, adding to the fisherman's difficulties. Here an accurate or lucky cast close to the rock will sometimes produce good-sized trout, but on the whole this part of the stream is one where numbers can be looked for rather than size. It is a stream less like a Perthshire burn than one of those which flow to the Tweed, and as we stand by the waterside looking upstream past the green haughs and windings of the May to the white shoulders of the hills at its head, we might be looking up Bowmont Water to the great rising face of Cheviot.

Pat's rod is up first and he turns to wait for me. The simple figure-of-eight knot by which the cast is tied to the line seems more difficult than usual, for my fingers are clumsy with haste and with the excitement of knowing that the burn is in splendid order ; but at last I am ready. We look at our watches to map out to best advantage the hours ahead, and then we face upstream. Immediately above us the burn makes a sudden turn under an outcrop of rock forming a pool, narrow and deep at the neck, but broadening out below. Except for the narrow neck, it is easily fished, and Pat, leaving it for me, goes a short way upstream before himself starting to fish.

Wading out into the rapid water below the pool, I let out my line, lengthening it by false casts till enough is out to reach the tail of the pool. Each of the first few casts brings rises, one to the tail fly, and sometimes a second to the dropper, but the eagerness and haste of the trout are as great as my own, and I fail to hook them. A trout rises in the centre of the pool with the head and tail rise which can be so deceptive of size, for what one sees may be the whole length of a small trout or only the head and shoulders of a much larger one. Convinced in my eagerness that it is the latter, I move forward a hurried step or two and cast again. As the flies fall, a very small trout rises nearer me at the dropper and I strike quickly and wildly. The trout flies through the air over my shoulder and becoming detached in mid-air, falls some yards behind. Hurrying back, I search desperately for it in the deep grass and return it to the water, grudging the waste of time and annoyed that the smaller trout has spoiled my chances of the larger one.

Straightening the line once more and returning to the point from which I made my cast, I start again. Now I can cover the whole of the broad part of the pool and a little backwater under the rock on the far side. Here, as the tail fly falls in the still water, a trout rises among the little specks of foam which spin slowly round in the eddy. As I strike, I feel the more solid resistance of a bigger fish and instead of jerking it through the air, I drag it splashing and kicking across the surface, to pull it safely, if rather anxiously, up on a little bank of shelving sand at my side. It is less than three ounces, but fat and firm, and beautifully marked. Killing it quickly, I wash it in the burn to remove the sand which sticks to its sides, and then slip it through the hole in the lid of my fishing-basket, a satisfactory foundation for the day's catch.

By now, the main part of the pool is much disturbed, and though I try a few more casts, nothing moves. But there remains untried the deep and narrow run under the rock face at the neck. I cast up into it, but time and again the west wind blowing down the glen catches my flies, and, try as I may, I fail to make the right allowance for its fitful strength. Finally, my cast is blown against the rock face. The tail fly catches on a tiny patch of moss, and only after a series of jerks straining the gut perilously near to breaking-point, does the fly come free. Reeling in the line, I walk up past the pool, keeping well back from it, and coming down again to the water's edge a few yards above I cast downstream into the neck. Now it is easier to control the line, and from where I stand I am casting away from and not towards the mossy face of the rock. The second cast goes right, and I draw the flies up against the strong stream of the neck, the dropper dancing and bobbing on the surface. Well up in the narrowest part of the run, a good trout comes right out of the water as he jumps at the dangling dropper, but misses it. I cast again quickly, and this time he takes it with a quiet and determined head and tail rise. He is too large to jerk from the water, nor is it possible to pull him upstream against the strong current. Instead, I let him go downstream into the body of the pool and getting below, land him on the same sandy bank where the first trout was landed. He is only just over a quarter of a pound, but a good trout for this upper part of the burn, and I leave the pool well satisfied with the start of the day.

As I turn upstream I can see Pat a little way ahead with fifty yards of unfished water between us. Beyond him my eye follows the burn as it runs through stretches of rushes and little green haughs, and here and there I can see ewes and their lambs grazing in the small patches of rich pasture formed by the bends of the stream. Farther still, the burn is visible only at intervals where shallow runs or tiny waterfalls catching the sunlight show as gleams of silver set in green. Then the burn bends out of sight round the base of a hill whose rounded shoulder shimmers as the sun's heat rises from the drying bents.

A few yards upstream is a long shallow pool, deepening gradually towards the neck where the water enters over a little fall. At the tail of the pool is a gravel bed in which patches of yellow mimulus are growing, and as I approach, a pair of sandpipers rise from it and fly upstream keeping close over the water and calling to one another as they go. In low water the tail of this pool would be too shallow to fish and only the deeper part near the neck would be worth a cast. But to-day the burn is full and I can see that even near the tail there is a narrow strip at either side where, close under the bank and overhung with a fringe of bents and rushes, the water is brown and deep enough to hold trout. But the wind blows straight down the stream with just sufficient strength to make accurate casting difficult. I cast up the pool again and again, but each time the wind baffles me as I try to aim the flies close under the banks. Often the flies are blown on to the bank from which I am lucky to recover them without finding them hopelessly caught in the round seed clusters of the rushes, and the best

I can do is to land them in the shallow centre of the water where there is little hope of a rise.

At last I give it up, and walking upstream I fish the pool down from the neck. Now I find that by drawing the flies upstream and slightly across the stream, it is possible so to manœuvre them that the current swings them in close to the bank and even under the overhanging grasses. In this way I get several rises, and two more trout which satisfy my not too exacting standard of size are added to my basket before the tail fly gets hopelessly caught in a rush and the pool is disturbed.

Above the long pool I fish on, catching trout in unexpected places, but failing where the chances seem greater. It is often so after a night of rain, perhaps because the trout in the smaller holes and corners now made fishable by the fresh water feel and welcome the change more than their more fortunate neighbours accustomed in the larger pools to a less changing depth of water. I pass many deep corners and backwaters ideal for the worm fisher, but too small even to-day for fly, and think with some regret of the Stewart tackle in my fly book and the worm tin in my pocket. But Pat and I have agreed to fish up some way farther with fly, and not for another couple of miles will I feel that honour has been satisfied and that I can change to the more homely familiar worm.

Soon I reach the point where Pat, now some way ahead, had started fishing, and reeling in my line, I walk up to overtake him. I find he has caught over a dozen trout to my seven, and all but one of them bigger than mine. I walk on some way ahead and start again. So we fish our way slowly upstream. The day gets hot and the level of the burn begins gradually to fall, but the trout continue to take well, and our baskets grow perceptibly heavier. Here and there we pass very small streams which feed the May from either side. In one of these before it falls into the main burn, I find a small deep pool quite unfishable with fly but so tempting that I shorten my line and adding a worm from my tin to the tail fly, pull out a very dark but good-sized trout from under the bank. There is a curious fascination in these little

84

side streams and their unsuspected pools ; in knowing that many of them have seldom been fished, and that the trout in them have lived, they and their ancestors, for many generations back, in these same pools, untroubled and unchanged by what is passing in the glen and on the hills around them.

As the morning passes, my standard of casting, never very high, begins to deteriorate. My whippy Greenheart rod is too heavy for constant casting into the wind and my wrist tires. More and more often the cast goes astray, landing among the rushes of the bank or on the stones. These last are a constant danger, for in the burns of the Ochils there are few pools where you will not find, in the centre of the stream, a rounded stone covered with a velvet cushion of light green moss and sometimes growing from it a tuft of tall feathery grass. Time and again I find my flies caught on such a stone, and in my haste I become careless, jerking at the cast and sometimes leaving the tail fly behind. Then I lay down the rod and hurriedly opening my fly book take out of it a tattered envelope containing a dwindling number of spare flies tied on gut. These have been carefully soaked the night before and have started the day twisted into the neat coils in which they came from Robert Turnbull's tackle shop in Edinburgh. But as the day goes on they become more and more disordered from my fatal habit of trying to extract a fly without troubling to undo the coil.

After a time Pat, who is some way ahead of me, stops where a rather larger stream enters the May from the south side, and as I overtake him he tells me it is lunch time. I am not sorry, and we sit down to eat our sandwiches on the south-facing slope of the hill above the burn, resting our backs against a shoulder of sun-warmed bents rising behind us. After lunch we share the chocolate which Pat has brought, and later lie gazing up into the blue expanse while the constant sound of the burn fills our hearing as we drift closer and closer to and finally across the borders of sleep.

When we wake again, and Pat starts off up the main burn, I yield to the temptation of fishing with a worm a short way up the side stream. The burn is very small but still run-

ning brimful, and in the many places where the turf comes
near to meeting over the water, the grass on the lip of either
bank is flattened and brushed downstream showing how high
the water has risen in the early hours of the morning. It is
easy fishing after my struggles to cast against the wind and
among the rushes of the main stream, and the readiness with
which the trout take confirms me in the belief that mine is
the first baited hook these pools have seen for many a day.

At a bend of the stream I pass from sight and sound of the
main burn into the utter quiet of the hillside. There is little
sign of life except for a pair of grey wagtails which move from
stone to stone ahead of me, showing as they do so the yellow
colouring which makes them seem so like the true yellow
wagtail more rarely seen in the Ochils. Even the sheep seem
to have deserted that little gully, till round a bend I come
to a steep little waterfall at the foot of which an old ewe
grazes in the rushes. Her back is towards me, and moving
quietly up, the sound of my steps drowned by the falling
of the water, I come close to her and drop my worm into the
pool by her side near where a mossy stone glistens from the
spray of the fall. The worm is immediately taken, and only
as a trout wriggling and twisting is pulled from the water and
deposited in the rushes does she raise her head and start
suddenly off, to turn at a little distance and stamp in the
sudden indignation which fright brings to animals and humans
alike.

Above the waterfall I try a few more pools, but here there
seem to be no trout, and making across the shoulder of the
hill I hurry to overtake Pat in the glen below. As I come
down the hillside I look up and down the stream. At first
I can see no sign of him, but at last I catch sight of him at a
bend a little way upstream and am not sorry to rejoin him,
for I am secretly not a little in awe of that quiet glen.

Late in the afternoon we come to a place where the burn
divides, one branch coming down a narrow gully on the north
side from behind the farm of Greenhill, while the other, the
main stream, leads on to the foot of the pass through which
we came in the morning. Both branches are now too small

for fly, so at their junction we change to worm and fish a little way up the smaller. By now the trout, gorged with the glut of worms and insects which the rain has brought to them, are taking rather less eagerly, but we get a few trout in the lower pools. Then we climb from the gully, pulling ourselves up the steep sides by the strong thick bracken which covers them, and crossing a stretch of bents, come down again on the main branch of the burn a little way below where it passes in a stone tunnel under the hill road to Dunning. We cross the road and enter a long meadow which stretches ahead for some distance.

Near its upper end the shepherd from the farm of Corb has started to cut with a scythe thatch for his few stacks of meadow hay, but for most of its length the meadow is deep in rushes. In the rather drier parts back from the burn grass of parnassus gleams, like white stars scattered through the green of the rushes, but beside the burn as we push our way up our feet sink in patches of mint and beds of water-cress. The tall rushes grow to the very waterside and some, beaten down by the rain, lean over the burn or lie trailing on its surface. Only here and there can we find more open spots into which to drop a worm and with our time now short we hurry on to the spring at the head of the burn. Here beside the path we sit for a few minutes to share the last piece of chocolate, to rest tired feet, to ease fingers cramped with hours of gripping the handles of our rods, and to count the four dozen trout which our baskets hold.

As we climb again westward through the pass, it seems to be steeper and narrower than it was in the morning. It is darker too, for up here under the highest of the hills we are near the level of the mist now beginning to drop down towards the tops which soon it will cover. Crossing the fence at the Coulshill end of the pass and seeing again the familiar view north-west to the Grampians, there is a vivid sense in my mind of passing from the strange and exciting back to the homely and familiar. Thoughts of home banished by the new surroundings of the past day come flooding back. We fish a few of the best pools of the Coulshill burn, but do not spend long, for it is late and we are tired, while ever more strongly grows in our minds the thought of supper in the nursery at Foswell.

Memories of the May recall other days when we fished not the head waters but the lower stretches. There is a rough and steep hill road which climbs the slope behind Dunning overlooking the little village with its square twelfth-century tower, its crooked streets and its old houses, once the homes of handloom weavers and poachers. At the top of the hill the road crosses a stretch of windswept moorland dotted with scattered whins, and leads in a mile or two to a point where a sudden twisting incline goes down to the valley of the May at Pathstruie. Sometimes we went this way, fishing our way upstream and so home past the meadows of Corb and Greenhill ; but more often we followed the main road through Dunning, reaching the May at a lower point where it runs through the woods of Invermay. Its lower course is in marked contrast to the miles of open hill and glen which lie upstream from Pathstruie. Here, as there, the glen is narrow and steep-sided, but instead of bents and bracken and scattered firs, the slopes immediately above the water are covered with a thick tangle of ash and hazel and alder. Upstream, the problem as one fishes lies in aiming the cast accurately into the small pools or the narrow parts of the wider pools where the water is of any depth. Down here the pools are mostly big and deep, but to manœuvre rod and line through bushes and trees and undergrowth and then to avoid overhanging branches as one casts, calls for the greatest care and patience.

Water is a supreme architect. It carves and shapes the rocks and banks of the riverside with an unapproachable artistry working slow change on the natural features which surround it, and adapting them to its design until they became at last essential and fitting parts of the whole. So the May has worked its quiet will in the glen among the woods below Pathstruie. Here and there as in the upper reaches, are bold outcrops of rock forcing the stream to a sudden turn, but so skilfully has the water adapted itself that rock and stream seem rather in alliance than in opposition, and the water hurries away on its new course leaving behind it for the fisherman a deep pool and tree-shaded eddy, a masterpiece of natural planning. The alder trees press close to the water's edge, sometimes overhanging it, often growing on its very banks, their roots thrust far down below the surface, forming an underwater trellis-work through which the stream eddies and sucks and behind which the trout have safe refuge. In pool after pool of the lower May you will find the alders jutting into the stream causing a rush of water and a deep eddy on the downstream side, while the lower branches hang down till they trail almost on the surface. As if to add to the fisherman's troubles, it often happens that the bank of the stream opposite is steep and rocky, throwing the current to the wooded side far under the hanging branches.

It was on a day in late summer many years ago that Pat and I first fished this lower part of the May. The growth of grass and leaf and plant was at its height, and beyond the trees, in a steep field on the west-facing slope of the glen, hill partridges called round the edge of the ripening oats. In the tangled thicket along the waterside I could do little but follow Pat, guiding my rod point as best I could among the maze of branches and tall grasses and wondering at the skill with which he cast his flies into pools overhung with trees. As we pushed our way upstream, quantities of tiny burrs stuck to our stockings from which in the evening Garry, a dog of strong character and unusual tastes, would nibble those which had clung there all through the long day.

Some way below Pathstruie is a pool typical of many in the May, but one which has always remained distinct in my memory. At its neck the water entered in a swift stream, deep and narrow under a leaning alder whose branches shaded and overhung the widening pool below. Pat waded into the stream some way above the pool, and coming cautiously down, cast his flies sideways into the deep neck of the pool under the tree, pulling them upstream against the current, while I kneeling well back from the bank, peered down through the thick branches. I can see the pool now and can hear Pat's sudden exclamation, " I've hooked a crocodile "— an event which in fact could hardly have caused me more excitement and astonishment than the subsequent landing of a trout of three-quarters of a pound, for a fish of such a weight from the burns was to me at that time quite unheard of.

A little way below Pathstruie the May enters a deep gorge. The almost sheer sides are covered with rowan and hazel which somehow find a precarious foothold in the rock-face, while out over them pigeons fly, and jackdaws from the holes near the upper edge of the gorge where they make their nests. We do not attempt the dangerous task of fighting our way up through the gorge, the deep black pools of which must, I feel sure, hold trout grown to monstrous size in an old age untroubled by hook or fly, but climb instead a steep slope of grass and bracken well back from the stream. Above the gorge, we come down steeply through tangled hazel and old hawthorns which overlook a long meadow where the May is joined by one of its main tributaries, the Chapel Burn, and here in the open meadow ground are pools more easily fished. To make up for the long stretches where I could only watch, Pat leaves these for me, and especially the pool where the Chapel Burn joins the May, a pool bordered by a bed of mint growing down to the water at the foot of a bank which in late summer scabious and harebells share with meadowsweet.

A short way above the point where the Chapel Burn joins the May, a stone bridge carries across the main stream the hill road from Dunning which here dips suddenly into the May valley to climb again on the south side over the hills to Milnathort. By the bridge stands the little group of houses known as Pathstruie.

When I first took the path along the glen past Pathstruie I knew nothing of the history of the place. I did not know that once it had been the centre of a community formed by all those little farms whose ruins I had seen on the sides of the glen, and for many more all through the surrounding hills ; that the waters of the May had once turned the wheels of lint and meal mills dotted at intervals along its banks, and that even then from the little post office at Pathstruie one could look across to a meadow in which could still be traced the ruins of what was once Struie Mill. I did not know of the stormy history of the little church which here looks down on the May from the hill on its south side, still less that almost within the memory of those then alive the banks of the Chapel Burn had on a Sunday in June in each year heard open-air sermons preached to many hundreds come over the hills from far and near—perhaps the last of the Conventicles. I knew only that here was a place whose quietness and beauty pleased me even while its remoteness awed me.

Since that first sight of Pathstruie I have come to know a little more of the place and of its history; of the men and women who lived there; of the old pack-man who, faced with ejection from his father's croft one hundred years ago, wrote in sadness and affection of the valley and its farms, of its pools and its streams by whose side he had so often walked. But this has brought me little nearer to understanding fully the fascination which the banks of the May have for me. It is a fascination as strong to-day and as indefinable as on those summer mornings at Foswell years ago when, wakened by the early chattering of sparrows in the laurels, I would open my eyes to see flies and casts soaking in readiness by my bedside, to recall that the previous evening Pat had charged Nurse, " If you're waking call me, call me early," to remember his bedtime promise, " To-morrow we will go to the May."

Chapter IX

THE LOCH IN THE WOODS

OF the entries in the diary where the results of my fishing
expeditions were for a few years recorded, some are
underlined while a few have earned the special distinction
of an asterisk. The latter badge of rank and quality has on
the whole been sparingly awarded. The sea-trout of Argyllshire share it with the big brown trout of Hampshire water
meadows, while occasional cold and largely barren evenings on
Loch Leven have, with a generosity which to-day I find surprising, been considered of equal merit. Of the other entries
distinguished in this way, one or two recur each year and stand
out far above the others, for they record days when the size
and weight of trout caught attained a level at that time far
beyond challenge. To few days during the whole of the fishing
season did I come to look forward with greater anticipation.
Seldom did they fail to come up to the high level of my expectation, nor was the frequency of their recurrence so great
as to blunt in any way the keenness of the pleasure which they
gave.

Far out in the strath, a ridge of gently rising ground lies
midway between the Ochils and the foothills of the Grampians.
It runs from the head-waters of the Allan, crosses the Earn a
little way upstream from the old bridge at Kinkell, and then

follows the north side of the river, to dip again to the valley of the Tay at Perth. It was along this ridge high above the marshes of the Earn that the Romans built their road leading from the big camp at Ardoch to the Tay valley, and here and there one may still come on pieces of old Roman cobbles and paving not yet completely overlaid by the road surfacing of more recent days. For most of its length the ridge is now cleared of timber and forms merely a great fold in the rich agricultural land of the valley, but as it nears Perth and rises to its greatest height it is tree-covered, and the road which the Romans made passes through a tract of heavily timbered country. Here the great Scots firs and the old larches rising from a carpet of blaeberry and an undergrowth of scrub birch are to-day a home for the roe deer, the woodcock and the capercailzie, a wild population perhaps not so very different from that which the Romans found. In the heart of this wooded tract lies a loch, and here, through the generosity of one of the best friends of my early fishing days, were spent the days recorded each season in my diary with all the honours and distinction which were rightly due to their outstanding excellence.

The first record in my diary of a day on the loch in the woods is dated 11th September 1913. I cannot at this distance of time remember that individual day, nor more than a few of those which followed in the coming years, but I can well recall the intense feelings of excitement and anticipation with which they were awaited, for those same feelings have been the prelude to each successive day on the loch. I recall the eager care with which on the evening preceding the expedition I would select a new cast from my fly book—for the old worn and patched ones used on our own loch or on the burns would never do—putting it to soak overnight in the soap-dish in the old night nursery where I slept. The patterns of flies used seldom varied much, a butcher on the tail with a grouse and claret and a teal and green as droppers. A calm day was now my greatest fear and when morning came my first care was to run to the window to look anxiously, and often in vain, at the tops of the trees for the least swaying of their branches.

From the main highway which runs to Perth a side road

leads to the loch, threading its way, grass grown and quiet, among great trees. On the larches and the Scots firs the bark is rough and lichen-covered with age and their roots are sunk deep in feathery moss growing on mould from the fallen leaves and needles of a hundred years and more. As one nears the loch, but before it comes in sight, some sense, perhaps of hearing, perhaps of lightened atmosphere but so subtle as to be almost below consciousness, tells of the nearness of the great opening in the trees ahead. Then the silver reflection of a broad sheet of water begins to appear through the tree trunks and in a few yards its whole expanse comes into view, while the sudden startled cries of the water-fowl echo across it.

Beside the thatched boat-house the keeper meets us. Sometimes if the morning is windless we reach the waterside before him, for he, wise man, knows from long experience that till a wind comes and flies begin to hatch fishing is almost useless. While we wait his coming we put up the rods and then sit looking over the smooth water to where far out the dabchicks dive, leaving on the surface little swirls and widening rings which, in my eagerness, I imagine to be the rings of rising trout. I grudge each moment spent on shore and sometimes my thoughts of the keeper are far from tolerant, for I do not think that it occurs to me that he has not, as I have, spent the last few days longing for the coming of this day.

Of the many days on which we fished the loch in the seasons which succeeded that first expedition in 1913, there were, of course, some on which, despite the sheltering ring of trees, a steady ripple covered its surface. Such days made few demands on the expert boatmanship of the keeper, for the loch is shallow and the trout cruise and feed over its whole area. Little more is then needed than to keep the boat drifting quietly before the wind which generally blows from the west end, and if one's attention does not wander too far from one's flies some measure of success is almost assured.

There are many distractions. The loch and its surroundings form a natural bird sanctuary. The reed beds round its edge are a home for every sort of water bird. The Great Crested Grebe sometimes breeds there, and there is never a day when the surface is not dotted with ducks of many kinds, some regular residents and some visitors on passage between the mud flats of the Tay estuary and the upper reaches of that river or the near-by Earn. Sometimes we would hear the tapping of the Great Spotted Woodpecker far off among the woods, and occasionally we saw it crossing the loch with laboured undulating flight ; but the most frequent distraction came from the second rod fishing from the opposite end of the boat. If a sudden rise to his flies were missed, there was, I found, the greatest temptation to watch his next cast to see whether the trout would come again. This was a fatal habit, for time and again it happened that a trout rising but missing his flies, continued its cruise across the line of the drifting boat to make its next rise to one's own cast, a manœuvre which constantly caught me unawares.

Of all these diversions the trout took the fullest advantage, to such an extent indeed that I came to wonder whether the wandering of attention was not sometimes the direct cause of the rise of a trout. I used to think then, and have often thought since, that when the eye and the mind are distracted from the flies, some sudden change or interruption in the action of the rod, some more natural movement of the flies in the water, may momentarily increase their attraction.

Productive as were those days when the breeze blew steadily from the west they were not, I think, the days I enjoyed the most nor were they those which, looking back, I think of as most typical of the loch in the woods. Far commoner and on the whole more interesting were the days when the breeze was light and fitful, sometimes dying to a flat calm broken only by the rings made by ducks drifting and dozing on its surface, by dabchicks busily diving, and by the tiny dimples made on the surface by feeding trout. Then and then only was it sometimes good policy to take one's eyes from one's flies and look around. On such days the trout seldom approached within short casting distance of the boat, nor was it very profitable or interesting to continue casting steadily into the calm water. Instead, we would watch for a trout rising within possible range, and while the keeper edged the boat softly and with infinite care in its direction, we would try with our longest and most delicate cast to drop the flies near where the trout had last risen.

Such long-range fishing had many drawbacks, but lack of interest was not one, and there was plenty of excitement. The days of light breeze and calms had another attraction, for on them one could study the manner in which so often these big trout fed on the surface, a manner which seemed to me peculiar to and typical of them ; for while a few would take a fly with the rush or the savage boil or the head-and-tail rise of more orthodox trout, the method of approach of the majority was very different. There seemed to be a certain quiet furtiveness in their rises as if they hoped, not always in vain, that their rise might be unperceived or as if they were shy of making some sudden movement which would reveal to the fisherman their great size. Time and again I have in calm water or in the lightest of ripples seen the surface stir almost imperceptibly, so that when one struck one did so tentatively rather than with confidence. Sometimes there might be the smallest break of the smooth surface or only the bare consciousness of some slight movement below the water, and after hooking a trout I have often tried in vain to cast my mind back and remember the manner and appearance of its rise.

In no other water which I have fished have I experienced more vividly the feeling of utter inadequacy, even of presumption, which these trout managed to convey. One felt that here hidden from the outer world they moved in majestic deliberation, in the shadow of great trees, through the luxuriance of waving water weeds and rustling reeds, among their neighbours the water fowl, taking their natural and rightful place in it all, disdainful, contemptuous and almost careless of intrusion on their sanctuary of wood and weed and water.

But if the rises of these trout were slow and deliberate, their reactions to the feel of the hook were quite the reverse. No sooner was the trout hooked than he would make one headlong dash out from the boat, tearing line off the reel and throwing himself again and again into the air with the headlong leaps of wild and desperate effort. Then, when many yards of line were out, there would often come a swift deep rush back to the boat, so sudden that there was no hope of reeling in the slack line or doing more than pull it in by hand, letting it fall loosely on the bottom of the boat, where as often as not it became tangled or got caught in one of the many angles or projections which seem to lie in wait for just such a contingency. Meantime the trout diving almost uncontrolled beneath the boat would make off behind one's back, the chances of the fight now heavily in its favour. One trout which dived below the boat did indeed throw away its excellent chance of escape by jumping into the boat behind my back, but a fair proportion of them made good the escape which their strength and subtlety had earned.

These big trout often played another very effective trick. A trout hooked near the stern of the boat would make a sudden and most determined rush towards the bow, with the apparent object of fighting its way round the bows and incidentally entangling itself with the line of the rod fishing at that end of the boat. Quite often this succeeded, and more than once the lines became so entangled that the bow rod became an unwilling and very unhelpful participant in the struggle. Bitter experience should have taught us that when a large and active trout is hooked by one rod, his companion can often best assist by suspending his own operations for a time ; but when one is young and keen and large trout are rising freely, this is a hard lesson to learn. The temptation for the second rod to continue fishing was often too great, and the experience of past disasters was apt to be ignored in the recollection of those memorable if less frequent occasions when two trout were successfully and almost simultaneously landed.

For many seasons we fished the loch once in the spring, generally in April, and once in the late summer. Of these days, the one in the spring was generally the more successful and almost always the more interesting. At the west end of the loch and for some distance along the north-west shore is a belt of rushes and marshy ground. Here, year after year, the gulls nest in great numbers, their nests built so close to one another that often it is difficult to tell where one nest ends and another begins. Indeed, one wondered whether the gulls themselves could always be sure that they were brooding their own and not their neighbour's eggs. The nesting gulls disturbed and dirtied the water round their nests, but they brought much food, too, and often if the boat were manœuvred carefully in to the very edge of the nesting ground there was a good chance of hooking some of the big trout which cruised in the shallow water almost among the nests, while the gulls in an indignant mob screamed and swooped overhead.

Near the north end of the loch was a small island. A few trees grew on it, rising from a dense mass of rhododendrons which covered its whole area and grew leaning out over the water on every side. Here each season a pair of wild swans made their nest. It was hidden deep in the heart of the rhododendrons and was formed in a huge mass of reeds and sticks and small branches, the accumulations of many nests of past years. Round the island the cock bird kept his watch, proud and suspicious, ready to warn off or fly hissing to the attack of any intruder, and even of such small ducks and dab-chicks as were bold enough to venture near.

One May day of light breeze and bright sun we had drifted close to the island. The breeze fell and we lay motionless, while the glare of the sun on the calm water made fishing tedious and almost useless. I had been amusing myself, as I often do when loch fishing on calm days, trying to see how accurately I could cast to a given spot on the loch's surface, to a floating leaf or a speck of foam. It happened that the swan approached the line of my cast only a few yards beyond where my flies were falling. The temptation to experiment on a live moving target was too great, and lengthening my line, I threw the flies across his path. As he swam over them I raised the rod and hooked him in the leg. The pull of the line or the feel of the hook can have been little more than a source of mild annoyance to him, and he swam on almost unconcerned, taking out my line with a quiet strength which could not be disputed. Alarmed now at my rashness, I put what strain I could on the line, and only then did the swan realize the connection between the boat and the pull on his leg. No sooner did this dawn on him than he turned and started to come quickly at us with very ominous intent. Turning the boat, the keeper rowed off with all his strength, and after a moment of great anxiety, the cast broke. As we rowed on to put a respectful distance between us and the outraged swan, we counted ourselves lucky to have emerged with the loss of no more than our dignity and a new cast.

My diary records few days on the loch when the results were not far above the standard attained on any other water which we at that time fished, and only on one occasion do I recall a completely blank day. The luxuriant growth of weeds along the shores and on the bed of the loch, while largely responsible for the abundant food supply on which those big trout thrive, has one peculiar disadvantage to the fisherman. As the summer goes on, there forms on the weeds a coating of some kind of vegetable growth. Later, under the action of wind and sun this becomes broken up and released into the water in the form of countless tiny particles, and in almost every season there is a period of a few weeks after midsummer when the water is so thick with these that fishing is almost useless. On one such day we fished the loch but found the water so thick that it soon became obvious that no trout could see the fly on the surface. The nearest we came that day to catching a trout was when one, cruising in search of food, swam close past the boat and almost on the water's surface. But even it failed to see the flies cast directly in front of it, an incident which forced me reluctantly to admit that there was no hope that day.

Of the size and weight of the trout which we caught on the loch in the woods it is difficult to write without seeming exaggeration. Just as our return empty-handed from the river was, at a later stage, to become almost a matter of course, so our return from the loch in the woods was looked for at Foswell with an expectation which was seldom disappointed, and as we came down the stairs into the kitchen, Annie beaming with pleasure, would fetch her largest ashet and dust with her apron the flour and crumbs from the top of the weighing machine which she well knew would be needed.

The entry which I made in my diary for 27th April 1917 recalls one day on the loch of which the memory is very vivid, though even it was not that on which the catch was greatest in number or in weight. We had wakened at Foswell to a morning of strong south-west gale. Up there on the hillside the wind was so strong that fishing seemed quite impossible, but we comforted ourselves by the thought of the sheltering wood round the loch and the hope that later in the day the wind would fall. When we reached the loch, its surface was for once white with spray and foam blown from the waves sweeping across it from the west end, and to launch the boat seemed almost impossible and certainly useless.

All morning we waited impatiently, for the loch can only be fished from a boat, till in the early afternoon a slight moderation of the wind made it seem at last possible to fish. The only part where there seemed to be the slightest chance of success was in a very narrow strip of water immediately adjoining the rushes and weeds and the gulls' nests at the extreme west end. The keeper forced the boat among the nests and rushes so that it was possible for us to cast out into the little strip of fishable water, keeping our rod tops low in the hope of avoiding the wind which every now and then swept the flies from the water as fierce gusts ran like black shadows scudding over the rough surface. As the day wore on, the wind moderated still further and more and more of the loch's surface became fishable. That day we had bicycled over from Foswell, and with a view to the ten-mile ride back against the strong west wind which still blew, we stopped fishing at four o'clock, taking ashore with us fifteen trout which weighed just over twenty-five pounds.

Where the quality of the day-time fishing was so high there was less temptation to fish on late, and even the keenness of a boy revelling in sport the like of which he experienced at no other time, came near satiety before evening; but once or twice we resisted the temptation to go early to the loch or stopped fishing in the afternoon, and returned later, and on these occasions we fished on till the light failed. On one such evening in July, we found the trout feeding steadily near the west end offshore from the gulls' nesting ground and the near-by belt of tall reeds. The breeze fell gradually to the faintest ripple, and at last to a flat calm which seemed to be the signal for the sudden awakening of all the wild life of the loch and the waterside. Now we could see trout feeding all round us, the waves and ripples made by them seeming monstrous on the smooth surface. In the middle of the reed bed quietly rustling close behind us, ducks moved and splashed, and with a sound like a great wind thousands of starlings rose from it and circled above us wheeling and swooping in perfect unison. Great trout were rising on every side, and for a time we could think of little else, but as the light failed making it more and more difficult to see the rises against the growing dark of the water in front, we turned and faced the west. Here the light of sunset slanting through scattered firs at the loch's edge had turned the smooth surface to a sheet of pale gold, and far overhead a rippling pattern of cirrus cloud was touched with the colour of fading rose.

Out on the Perth road on our homeward way we pass between the black walls of big fir plantations from which comes the cool damp smell of dew fallen on sun-warmed woods. Where it leaves the trees the road starts to fall gradually into the valley of the Earn. Below us the hollow is filled with soft twilight through which comes the reflection of water as the bends of the river catch the last of the light. Fields and trees and woods merge into a deepening shadow which slowly obliterates the landmarks of modern times, till all that remains is old, quiet and unchanging—the dark valley, the gleam of water, and beyond, the soft outline of the Ochils.

CHAPTER X

GLENETIVE

THE memories and impressions of early childhood are for
me blessedly and inextricably entangled with Argyllshire and the shores of Loch Etive. Few places to-day have
a greater power to start in my mind the threads of far-away
recollection, threads leading often from nowhere to nowhere,
tantalizing scraps of memory in isolation. Sometimes they
are only fleeting impressions without continuity, and almost
I would think without any reality were it not for the knowledge that for one small point of time they have deeply stirred
the memory and the emotions. The mists of time and distance
seem in that instant to have parted to give a thrilling glimpse
back to childhood, but as I look the mists close again before
the focus of the mind's eye has allowed me to take in the details
of the view, or even to become more than dimly aware of what
I have seen. Perhaps the colour and outlines of our memory
pictures, faded through age, are too delicate for clear perception or like the smallest stars elude our vision when we gaze
directly at them, only to mock us with a sudden and unexpected glimpse of their brightness as the eye turns away.

Before you come to Achnacloich station on the side road
which leads from Stonefield, you pass a small white gate in
the roadside dyke from which a path winds uphill through
oak woods. It is a path on which in early summer one seems
to wade through a mist of blue as the wild hyacinths spread
on either side in a flood among the trees and up to their very
trunks. From the path one looks down through the oaks to
a little bay below the station, a bay which seen between the
branches of the trees forms, I believe, the earliest picture of
which my mind keeps the memory. Here miscellaneous pack-
ages, piles of coal and drums of oil used to stand at the pier
end waiting to be shipped to their destinations across the loch
or up to the glen at its head, and in the planks of the pier were

chinks through which one could catch the flash of sunlight reflected in the silver and brown of the water moving below. At the far side of the pier steps led down to the water for use at low tide, and from a precarious perch near the foot of them, slippery with seaweed and salt water, I watched my brothers and sister fish for the cuddies and little crabs which moved among the great timbers of the pier or on the bottom of the loch.

Achnacloich pier was the home of a little steamer called the *Ossian*, at least I suppose she was little though in those days she seemed to me enormous. Every day, except Sunday when she lay at the pier, the *Ossian* did the trip to the head of the loch and back under the command of a grey-bearded seaman who had the reputation of knowing the west coast of Scotland inside out. The time came when instead of watching the *Ossian* disappear up the loch, I went in her, and so began for me a succession of visits which were to continue for many years and during which links of memory and affection were formed so close and strong that even to-day the influence of Glenetive on my mind and imagination seems as powerful as ever.

The sea lochs of the Scottish west coast have much to stir the imagination of a child, and of them all few can have greater fascination than Loch Etive. Here are mysterious currents, eddies and little whirlpools caused by the great rush of the tide over the Falls at Connel; the Narrows at Bonawe where the flow of a great incoming river is added to that of the salt water; the rising bulk of Cruachan to the south disclosing as one goes up the loch the rocks and precipices where the hill falls sheer to Glen Noe, and then the rounding of the bend beyond which the loch tapers before one as it stretches far into the heart of remote and towering hills.

The many journeys I have taken up that loch in later years have done little to detract from the feeling of insignificance and awed alarm with which on these early visits I stood on the deck of the *Ossian* and felt myself carried farther and farther among the rising hills. As we neared the head of the loch, we could distinguish the pier, and later the waiting dog-cart with Sandy Campbell the red-bearded ghillie, wearing the hard grey-green tweeds made from the wool of Glenetive sheep which all the Glenetive men wore. As I walked down the gangway on to the pier, I seemed to be entering a strange and exciting land where shapes and colours and smells had a significance and vivid intensity lacking in the world outside.

Leaving our heavy luggage on the pier to follow behind in a farm cart, we climbed into the waiting dog-cart and set off up the narrow road to Glenetive, the wheels crunching on the fine granite gravel among which particles of quartz sparkled in the sun, the horse's hooves falling with soft thuds into the loose sand between the ruts where grass and even little scabious grew undisturbed by the infrequent traffic. Above us on our left rose the slope of Ben Treallachain and far up on its shoulder wet rocks catching the sun made patches of black and silver set among the green of the rich tall grass. The dog-cart rumbled over the loose planking of the bridge at the post office under which the Galachulain Burn ran down to the loch, crystal water falling over sharp ledges of pink granite into ice-clear pools. Then came a small patch of alders and poplars and beyond them the road followed the river bank through a meadow of bog-myrtle to the foot of the avenue which sloped up through Scots firs and a thick undergrowth of tangled rhododendrons to Glenetive House.

With all its tremendous influence on the imagination and emotions of a child, the glen was far from being an ideal playground. There were no roads other than the seemingly endless one which stretched away up the glen towards the high hills above Dalness ; nor were there many paths, and to wander from the few there were was to find oneself involved in thickets of tall bracken and bog-myrtle growing in soft wet ground.

For a child just learning to fish the position was little better. I can remember only one small burn near the house, running through peat bog overhung with luxuriant bog-myrtle and brambles. Here were a few small trout, but they were hard to catch in the overgrown pools. For the rest, the burns were mostly big streams coming down the side glens in rocky gorges or beds filled with great smooth granite boulders, the water falling over successive ledges into deep clear pools. Into some of the lower pools sea-trout later in the season would struggle up from the main river. Apart from them, and despite my early conviction that great monsters lived in their depths, I think it is probable that these big pools held only very small trout, for the rocky sides and granite boulders gave scanty cover and the clear water held little food.

In the main river we seldom fished in these early days. The pools were much too big and deep and rocky, and the only fishing I can remember doing in the river was the dangling of a salmon fly over the high bridge at Coinlettir to see the parr come splashing up to it out of the awesome blackness of the still pool between the rocks below. At the foot of the avenue was the Cobble Pool, deep under the small alder bushes of the near bank and shelving to a gravel bed on the far side. Here sea-trout and finnock always lay and one could see them moving up and down the pool in an uneasy shoal in bright weather when the water was low and clear. Near the neck was moored

the small boat which gave the pool its name. Here we sometimes crossed to the flat ground on the far side which stretched
for half a mile to the whitewashed cottage at Kinlochetive
close in under the shadow of Ben Starav. On the flat were
rabbits among the bracken, and as one neared the head of
the loch, one would come on brackish pools where very small
fish stirred up the mud of the bottom as they darted for cover
on our approach.

On other days we would walk up the path beside the
river where the bracken grew tall under the oaks and alders
by the waterside, and fat black brambles grew on bushes
overhanging the little burns or climbing up the sides of the
loose dykes of mossy granite stones. The unusual luxuriance
of growth here in the moist softness of the west, of moss and
bracken and bramble, of birch and alder and hazel strengthened the impression of a new and strange country and the
feeling of excited anticipation which it brought. The blackness of pools by the roadside or in the river played its part,
while the sight of Loch Etive stretching into the distance and
the smell of seaweed at low tide gave the added hint of vast-
ness and mystery needed to complete a magic spell.

A little way up the glen past the house, screened from the
road by a beech hedge, was the garden, and here under the
shadow of Craig Dubh, Scott the tall bearded gardener reigned
supreme. Granite gravel paths edged with low hedges of
box ran between herbaceous borders where phlox grew
luxuriantly. Its scent filled the place and has to this day a
magical power of bringing to my mind the picture of the
Glenetive garden. I can see now the view through the birch
trees at its eastern end up the glen to Dalness and the twin
peaks of the Buchaille Etives, with the flat rocks of Coinlettir
to the south glistening in the sun against the green of the hill's
shoulder. I can see Scott standing beside the gooseberry nets,
rubbing the side of his face where an over-anxious midge has
got entangled in the hairs of his beard, expressing, as he does
so, on a variety of topics opinions whose originality is made
more startling by the misuse and mispronunciation of words
which to him seemed second nature.

After a time these early visits to the glen came to an end and for a few years I did not see it. Then about 1911 or 1912 I went there again with Pat and continued to go every summer for some years. By now I had reached the age when scenes and objects remembered from early days had entered the realm of reasoned and conscious perception. This did not lessen in any way the influence Glenetive exerted on my imagination. The impressions of early childhood had laid the foundations of this and nothing could or did affect it ; but now I could see and appreciate in detail those things which before only went to produce an indefinable but powerful emotional force. As the motor launch which had replaced the old *Ossian* moved up the loch, I saw more clearly the beauty of the shores, the shapes and colours of the hills, and the curves of the sandy bays ringed with pale gold drowsing in the quiet of an August day.

On such days the surface of the water was glassy calm, and looking up the loch a mirage seemed to dazzle the sight till from a distance one could not tell where the green of the points and promontories ended and the silver reflection of the water began. Beyond the Point at Barrs, the hazel wood which runs from the shore up the slopes of Ben Treallachain came in sight, the whole length of it in view from the Point up to near Glenetive pier. Far up on the hillside under the rock face the trees thinned till only a few scattered ones clung to the steep slopes, looking from the loch no bigger than small bushes. One day when we had rowed down from Glenetive, we climbed through the wood and up a dry water-course into the big cleft in the rock which runs to the top. The length and difficulty of the climb showed how deceptive to the eye is the view from the loch side, but our climb and the torments of the midges and the heat of that south-facing gully were rewarded, for coming suddenly to the top we disturbed an eagle which flapped clumsily up almost at our feet.

Across the loch the sides of Ben Starav sweep in a graceful curve down to the water's edge. As one comes up the loch it seems that the hillside is scarred with broadening lines of light colour on its dark surface, looking in the distance as if trails of lace were draped from its top, fanning out over the skirts of the mountain as they sweep down to the loch side. A nearer view shows how burn tracks starting as narrow rocky scars near the top gradually widen out as the slope becomes less steep into tracks of granite stones, grey and pink, and then into little deltas of loose boulders among the heather of the lower slopes. Down these in dry weather spring water trickles on the rock face and splashes among the boulders. Rowing far out on the loch on a still day, one hears all down the shore the small sound of falling water from the hillside, but the streams are invisible unless looking closely one can catch the sparkle of clear water falling between granite boulders at the loch's edge.

From these later visits comes a clear recollection of the details of Glenetive House. As one came in through the front door which faced the fir woods of Craig Dubh, one stepped into a stone-paved hall, treading on mats of deer-skin whose edges curled up to show the raw hide below, while round the walls just below the ceiling was a frieze of stags' horns. Beyond the hall was the smoking-room, the centre of the life of the house, where armchairs and one rocking-chair faced the marble-topped mantelpiece. On it stood a much-enduring barograph, and there were few hours of the day when one member of the party was not glaring at it in indignation as it quietly drew its upward-tilting line presaging drought and east wind, fatal alike to river and hill. Across the room were rows of old leather-bound periodicals, the Badminton library and the Fur, Feather and Fin books, and among a miscellaneous collection a copy of Bromley-Davenport's *Sport*, a book which at that time I had seen nowhere else. Each summer I read there the chapter which tells of the loss of the great salmon in the Rauma River at the head of Romsdal Fjord in Norway, and to the fascination of the book was added the thrill of my surroundings as I read on a Sunday afternoon sitting on the window seat of the library, the sound of the distant river coming to me through the open window.

The library windows faced south across the lawn, and gave a view over the tops of the Scots firs surrounding the house in which a ride had been cut to allow one to see down to the river. Each morning it was the habit, "duty" would perhaps be a better word, of each male member of the party to look through the big telescope which stood on a tripod in the window recess. For myself it was always to the river that I looked first, only to see it morning after morning a sad trickle among the stones. But beyond the river and tilting the glass far up, one looked to the great shoulder of Coinlettir and the conical peak of Glas Bein Mhor rising above the deep corrie down which the Coinlettir Burn ran to join the river at the head of a sea-trout pool. Sometimes we could pick out deer quite low down on the shoulder of the hill before the flies and the heat of the day had driven them higher. More often we would see them far back silhouetted against the skyline and moving among the granite slabs and boulders where the ptarmigan croaked.

No-one could stay at Glenetive without realizing very quickly how much the life of the house, if not of the whole glen, centred on the forest, and indeed by late August and early September when we generally went there, I had reluctantly to admit that the fishing, though by no means over, was getting past its best, while the stalking was just coming into its own. It was for this that the glass was watched so anxiously at night and the telescope turned up to the hill each morning. For this the daily concourse round the porch at the side door when we stood on the lawn and I tried to look wise and longed only for the river, while John Anderson, the head stalker, stood with his long weather-beaten face tilted to the sky, his eyes screwed up with the effort of concentration as he tried to detect some definite movement in the slowly drifting clouds overhead. Nor could anyone undergo or even listen to the searching examination by means of which in the evening every detail of the stalk was extracted from the men returned from the hill without knowing that here was the centre of interest.

But for me it was always the river, from the moment I stepped on to the launch at Achnacloich till the time when on the return journey, almost in tears with despair and home-sickness for the things I was leaving, I watched Glenetive recede over the boiling green of the launch's wake and finally disappear from view as we rounded the bend above Bonawe.

Captain Dawson, who had been translated from command of the *Ossian* to that of the Glenetive launch, was never communicative about the river on the way up the loch from Achnacloich at the start of our visits, refusing to be distracted from concentration on his course up the middle of the loch. As for the chauffeur who acted as engineer, all the information I could extract from him, shouting down the throb and clatter of crude-oil engines at full speed, was almost worse than useless to a boy eager to be told the full details of what had been caught and in which pools, and to know the exact height of the river.

As we made our way up the loch I would watch all the burns which came down the hills on either side for any sign of the white streaks which would tell me they were in spate. Each night at Glenetive I would lie awake for a time listening for the sound of rain. Sometimes waking in the darkness, I would think I heard it falling, but always it was the wind moving in the tops of the Scots fir wood which stood round the house. I remember on such occasions my feelings of bitter rage and the conviction that the Fates of malicious intent were cheating me of the spate I wanted so much. Morning after morning I looked eagerly, but without much real hope, through the smoking-room telescope at the river, and no "royal" unprotected by hinds on the side of Coinlettir would have been to me such a welcome sight as flood water covering the gravel beds above the Cobble Pool.

Looking back on these Glenetive visits, and indeed on much of our fishing in the west, I am astonished to recall how seldom we enjoyed even moderate rainfall during our holidays. Indeed, I can only recall one holiday, in Skye, when we had enough rain and then we had so much that the burns and rivers were in a constant state of enormous flood which made them practically unfishable. So even then Fate managed to defeat us. August is normally one of the wet months of the year on the west coast, and Glenetive, surrounded on every side by high ground rising often to 3,500 feet, has a very high annual rainfall, but it almost always happened that the weeks I was there were dry. Certainly there was one day when the Fates, seeing me start off down the loch in the launch for Achnacloich, thought it safe to send rain. That day the launch broke down and by the time it had limped back with me to Glenetive, the burns were already white on the side of Coinlettir, so that by evening the river was in order and the sea-trout rose well.

Of other rainy days in Glenetive I can only recall two. On one of these, though the river was in order and the pools nicely rippled by a mild west wind, it was decreed that I go to the hill, and all through a long stalk among the granite boulders of Coinlettir where rock-roses and stagshorn moss grow among beds of lichen, I saw in fancy the quick rush of the sea-trout and the slowly gathering wave of the rising salmon in the tails of the pools which I longed to be fishing. On the other day we had come down the glen from Rannoch through blinding mist and driving rain, and in the rocky gorge above Dalness the river roared in huge flood. All that night it rained, but by morning the sun was out and the river was falling to fishing level. We motored up to fish the top beat and found pool after pool in perfect order, but lashed by an upstream wind which all that day turned back and tangled the line till the back was tired and the spirit broken and despair came on us.

Constant low water drove us to many expedients. Sometimes we went down to the pier, and taking a row-boat fished along the shore beside the hazel woods of Ben Treallachain, or across on the Ben Starav side. If the river were low and sea-trout had accumulated round its mouth, we often did well fishing like this with ordinary loch or sea-trout flies along the edges of the seaweed offshore ; but though they were unproductive, the days I like almost best to remember are those when the breeze failed us, and landing for lunch below Ben Starav we lay in the heather, hearing the distant sound of water falling down the hillside above us, looking across to Ben Treallachain mirrored in the still water of the loch and up over the sandy river mouth into Glenetive.

There were mornings, too, when we forced ourselves to get up hours before breakfast, and slipping out of the side door with our rods, hurried across the lawn to the path through the woods. The effort of early rising is often rewarded, if by nothing else by an added keenness of perception of the things around one. When the mists of sleep have cleared away, the senses seem to emerge clearer and more receptive than usual. Perhaps from some quality in the early light and the unfamiliar angle of the shadows, objects around us seem sharper in outline and clearer to the eye. The sense of smell is keener, the hearing more acute if only because of the utter stillness common in the early hours. So it was on these early morning expeditions at Glenetive. Among the bracken and bog-myrtle by the riverside the spiders' webs were picked out in white and silver beads of dew, the big pools lay still, while over the shallows the streams talked on quietly as they had talked through the night. But lovely as these mornings were we seldom caught much, and often as the sun came up we were driven from the river by the midges which, unfortified by breakfast as we were, we found insufferable.

Looking back on it now, I often wish that we had experimented more with evening fishing. But days of stalking or fishing at Glenetive were hard days, the distances were long, and after dinner we were glad to sit half asleep before the smoking-room fire thinking over again the day on hill or river, or perhaps not thinking very much at all. Sometimes I liked to sit by the window looking out into the night, to feel the contrast between the warmth and light of the room and the shadows of the woods and the great hills outside. As the eye grew accustomed to the dark, one could see the hunched shapes of the rabbits as they nibbled and hopped on the lawn, while against the glass moved a grey mist of gnats and midges.

Glenetive in the days I knew it had no electric light and at bedtime we each chose a candlestick from the row placed on the hall table. At the corner landing half-way up the stair I would stop to watch the reflection in the glass against the black of the night outside, while fluttering bats or flighting woodcock looking in would have seen the yellow lights mounting slowly, one by one, to dwindle and disappear down the long passage. Often my bedroom faced to the north and across the avenue into the black wall of the Craig Dubh woods, but sometimes I had a room looking to the south.

One year we were there at full moon. Sitting at night on the window ledge I looked out over the tree tops and across the river. The great corrie opposite and the whole glen seemed filled with a silver haze of moonlight, across which here and there the hills threw shadows of jet. The outline of Glas Bein Mhor was clear against the sky and the rock slabs on the side of Coinlettir showed gleaming reflections through the haze. There was no wind or life or movement in the whole glen, and only the sound of the river came up to me from the distance. The sight was so overpowering in its beauty that after a time I turned almost with relief to the cosiness of the candle-lit room, taking with me, though I did not know it, the memory and inspiration of such a vision as Belloc saw when from the height of Weissenstein he viewed the distant Alps —one of those which " link one in some way to one's immortality."

On alternate Sundays during the summer the whole population of the glen walked to attend the service held by the young minister who the previous evening had come over the hill from Glen Ure at the head of Loch Creran. These were young theological students not yet ordained and in the glen they were commonly referred to as " missionaries." The name was not inappropriate, and I can imagine that crossing on stormy nights over the high pass between Ben Sguliaind and Ben Fhionnlaidh they may well have felt that they were coming to wrestle for the salvation of souls in darkest heathendom, an impression which must have been strengthened in the mind of one young student who, on questioning Scott as to the spiritual welfare of the glen, received the answer, " Church matters in this glen are a thing of the bypast, a mere vision of history."

Three miles up the glen a little schoolhouse stands in the angle formed by the river and a big burn which comes down

from the hills on the north side through a deep rocky gully hidden in hazel and birch ; and here the services were held. Inside the tiny classroom the seating was strained to its farthest limits, a circumstance which may have inspired the choice on one memorable Sunday of the text " . . . . and there was no room in the inn." Long-legged ghillies sat cramped in infant desks, failing attention found rival attraction in maps and the multiplication table, and between the verses of the psalms the sound of the river came through the open door.

In the afternoons of these Glenetive Sundays we would often climb Craig Dubh, up the steep track which zigzags between rocky outcrops and granite boulders lying among long grass under the Scots firs, and on past the water-supply tank with its corrugated iron roof, which, when I was small, I always imagined to be what people called the " watershed." As we neared the top, the fir trees became scattered and stunted, and now there was more thick grass and some rank bell heather with big fat " woolly bear " caterpillars and sometimes exciting green ones with red spots, and shiny brown parchment cocoons in the grass. Through the tree tops at our back, more and more of the glen and the distant river stretched in bird's-eye view below us, while to the west Loch Etive lay broad and silver, narrowing in the distance till it disappeared round the bend under the shadow of Cruachan. Beyond the top of Craig Dubh is a wide expanse of rough hillocky ground which stretches up to the foot of Ben Fhionnlaidh, the rank grass turning from green to orange as the summer passes. Here on the summit we lay, sleeping, spying the opposite hillside, or watching the high clouds drifting over the Glen Ure hills, as our fancy pleased us.

And now that I have written down some of the things I remember about Glenetive, and have tried to describe the glen and what it meant to me, I know that none of it can succeed in conveying the picture which I so much want to paint ; not just the appearance of the place, for anyone who goes there can see for himself the graceful sweeping lines of Ben Starav, how the mist hangs and clings and trails on the side of Coinlettir, or how in the sunlight the wind chases the cloud-shadows on the side of Ben Ceitlein and in the big corrie between the Buchaille Etives. No, what I want to do is to capture and put into words the thrill which still comes to me when I smell phlox in a garden, or box hedges, or the smoke of an extinguished candle ; when I hear music first heard in the Glenetive smoking-room, or the crunch of cart wheels on granite gravel. But that I cannot do.

CHAPTER XI

KILMARONAIG

A SHORT way to the west of Achnacloich, a low white-washed house stands among beech trees on a rise over-looking Loch Etive. From the drawing-room windows you look down a clearing in the trees and out across the water to Ardchattan and the hills behind Inveresragan, while from the other side of the house you can see down the loch past Connel to Dunstaffnage Bay and over to Mull. Here, in the white house for a number of years my grandmother spent each summer and autumn, and almost every year my cousin and I as very small boys spent part of our summer holidays with her.

The journey from Perthshire to Connel, the station for Kilmaronaig my grandmother's house, was to me at that time something of an adventure. Where the Callander and Oban line branches off the main Perth line at Dunblane, I waited for my connection, and heard with a thrill of nervous excitement the voice of the stout red-faced porter shouting, as the train came in, a long string of far-sounding names, giving to the last syllable of Oban, as he ended the catalogue, an emphasis appropriate to the terminus of the line.

This annual visit to my grandmother was then the only occasion on which I travelled up the Oban line, and the scenery had all the thrill of novelty added to its extreme beauty. As far as Callander the country, though strange to me and lovely, was still of the familiar east-coast agricultural type. It was early August, and the blue mist of wild hyacinths had long since faded in the woods round Deanston and the pale gold had gone from the broom banks by Doune. But at Callander the whole countryside changed. As the train left the station and crossed the bridge over the Teith it was as if we had come into a new land, and soon we were among the woods of the Pass of Leny where stunted oaks and twisted birches growing among moss-covered boulders spoke of the west country as surely as the bog-myrtle which now appeared on either side. The ground rose as we came under the shoulder of Ben Ledi, and all at once we were among the hills. Lochs and rivers and burns were all about, and, to the discomfort of my fellow-passengers, I gazed now from one window and now from the other as we crossed and recrossed the Leny, and then ran beside Loch Lubnaig so close that it seemed we must topple in, and up past the soft green meadows of Strathyre to Balquhidder.

As we toiled up Glenogle above Lochearnhead, the line seemed to be perched precariously among the huge hanging boulders of the hillside, an impression strengthened in later years by seeing from the road across the glen how slender are the viaducts and bridges on that piece of the line and how vast the masses of rock perched on the hillside above. The long stretch of Glen Dochart seemed interminable, but there were burns to watch and often one would see grouse or black-game perched on heathery hillocks near Luib. Even to-day this can be a wearisome part of the journey, and sometimes, going up that line at night and drowsing over a book I have wakened convinced that we must be nearing Connel, only to realize from the slow click of the wheels on the metals that we are still climbing up the incline towards the summit.

After Tyndrum the rhythm changed and quickened. In Glenlochy I would search the skyline to the north for deer, or watch in vain for fishable pools in the clear shallow little river now running to Loch Awe. Beyond Dalmally one thrilling sight succeeded another in breathless succession, the crossing of the Orchy at the end of Loch Awe ; the rich lush meadows at the river mouth where herons fish in reed-covered pools ; the view of Kilchurn Castle standing on its promontory looking out over shoal water from which tree stumps and branches washed down by winter floods lift great crooked limbs and roots like sea monsters. Where the line curved again westward to follow the shore of Loch Awe, one looked into the great corrie behind Cruachan and up to the rock wall which rises so steeply to the ridge. Soon we were among the moss and fern of the hazel woods where the side of Cruachan falls to the loch, seeing the quick flash of black and white in the depth of a green gully and hearing the sound of splashing water from the big waterfall on the Cruachan Burn.

Now came what was for me the great thrill of the journey. The loch began to narrow and the hills on its far side to close in. The water changed from blue to grey and then to black, and out of the reach of the breezes of the open loch it lay quiet and sinister in the Pass of Brander. While the train twisted and turned on the line above the water, I gazed down with horrified fascination to see the bottom of the loch plainly visible under the surface for a few feet from the shore, and then suddenly disappearing into the black of what I was convinced were bottomless depths below the hills. As the pass narrowed, little eddies started to appear on the surface of the water, then more and more, and at last came the rush of the stream from the stillness of the loch into the first pool of the river with the great back-water on the far side where the fishing-platform runs round the rock face.

Few salmon rivers in Scotland can rival in strength and speed the Awe as it sweeps down the few miles to Loch Etive. Between Loch Awe and the deep pools near the railway bridge three miles downstream is hardly a yard of quiet water, and a strong determined fish hooked on the upper part of the river has little to stop him below. My first sight of the Awe was in the days when narrow wooden platforms ran out into the tail of some of the broader pools, and I would sometimes see men standing on them far out over the stream casting fearlessly from their giddy perches. Since then I have met some of these men and know that their apparent courage did not reflect their true feelings in the matter, and that but for the presence and persuasion of the ghillie they would have remained in more secure if less advantageous places.

Below the railway bridge the river takes its first rest since leaving the loch, and as the train crossed, one could get a glimpse of black water swirling far below in the deep eddies of the Cassan Dubh. Then the line keeps round the hill face away from the river, but sometimes when the water was high I could catch a far glimpse of white under the beeches above Inverawe and could imagine the smooth water at the tail of the Cruive Pool quickening and sloping steeper and more steeply to break at last into the great white-crested waves of the rush down into the pool below. The last few miles were a rising tide of excitement. At Achnacloich I would lean from the carriage window to see the pier through the trees, with perhaps the *Ossian* waiting to leave for Glenetive, and to smell the salt of the shore and the delicate sweetness of the birch. Then up the incline we climbed through the cuttings between which I watched eagerly for glimpses of the bays and islands of the loch, and on at last to Connel.

My grandmother had in those days a most useful lad who helped with odd jobs round the house. He lived in a room above the garage and his time seemed to be divided between bringing in garden supplies to the house, raking the granite chips on the paths, and helping in the garden which lay to the south of the house, a great circular depression in the ground sloping from all sides to a rose-bed in the centre. Peter Farquharson had, to our minds, many excellent qualities. He could row a boat, he had a great sense of humour, and as we discovered later, considerable tact, and when he cared he could make his eyes turn inwards to look at his nose, a delightful trick which we never tired of asking him to perform. Perhaps it was as well that we were there only for a short time in the summer, for otherwise Peter's eyes might have become permanently deranged.

During our stay Peter's other activities were largely suspended and he became our official ghillie. Each morning he came round to the front door to find out what our plans were for the day. There was seldom much doubt about them, and as soon as our sandwiches were ready we would set off under the chestnut trees and through the farm steading to the old grass-grown road which led to the lochs in the hills. We must have been an odd trio, Peter going on ahead carrying the lunch, my cousin and I, probably wearing oilskins and sou'westers—for rain was never far away if only the soft drizzle of the west—lagging behind, planning where we would fish, arguing about trout caught or lost on other days, and then running on to catch up the long-suffering Peter, and both simultaneously appealing to him for confirmation of completely contradictory statements.

I think I can see every yard of that road. The rock under the railway bridge where the wild strawberries grew ; the beds of flags beside the slow peaty stream where the willows were rank and tall ; the peat bog where bog-myrtle and cotton grass grew round a little burn which our imagination peopled with trout of an immense and most improbable size. I can see the places in the road where little trickles splashed down through the fern from the rocky face of the rising ground on our right, to seep across the road through a trail of loose stones with scabious and butterwort and sundew growing in the damp ground at the road's edge. Then the way sloped upwards through bracken and heather, and from the top of the rise we looked down on the chain of lochs which was our goal, my cousin and I racing ahead of Peter to get the first sight of them. From where we stood we looked down on the nearest loch lying almost at our feet within its inner ring of water-lilies behind which were banks of tall reeds. In the middle distance the loch narrowed beneath a low hill covered with oaks and hazels, and beyond this again in the farther distance we could just see the gleam of the second loch.

On the road up our main anxiety was whether there would be a ripple on the water. The leaves of birch and hazel had been watched for the slightest movement, and each smallest sway had been hailed as showing the approach of the wind which we knew was so vital to the day's prospects. Sometimes the lochs sparkled and glittered as the westerly breeze blew down them lapping against the water-lilies which danced and bobbed on the rippled surface. Their wet leaves flashed in the sun, and the soft brush of the wind in the reed tops came faintly up the hill. But more often the sunlight was mirrored on calm smooth water, and the reflection of the big boulder which showed above the surface of the bay at the near end was as clear and sharp as the great stone itself.

Gladdened by the sight of the ripple, or fighting back our disappointment at the calm, we hurried down the slope to the boat-house built into the hillside below us, its back hidden in blackthorn and brambles. Our boat rode among the reeds, moored to her buoy a few yards out from the shore. While Peter pulled her in and baled the water which had leaked into her or had collected from showers in the night, we opened the boat-house and selected oars and rowlocks from the collection which shared the boat-house with landing-nets and boat-hooks, tea kettles and tins of paint and all the paraphernalia of past fishing expeditions and picnics. Then we would set up our rods at the water's edge, the dead reeds and flotsam of the winter storms cracking under our feet, while big blue and green dragon-flies sailed and flashed among the reeds, their wings as they passed making loud whirring noises like cheap mechanical toys unwinding in their flight.

There was often some discussion as to who should fish from the bow and who from the stern, over-conscientious effort at unselfishness on both sides threatening a deadlock. Actually there was little to choose, for while the stern rod may have had an advantage at times as we drifted along the edge of the water-lilies, the man in the bow had all the fun of casting ahead into the little patches of open water as Peter forced the boat through the reeds or up the narrow channel which connected the two lochs. The problem was usually solved on Peter's suggestion by our agreeing to change ends at lunch time, and soon we were heading for the open water, pushing through the scattered reeds and the water-lilies, whose wet leathery leaves slapped and squelched against the boat's sides as we passed.

The lochs are fed by springs and by one or two small burns full of very little trout, burns which run down through the surrounding oak woods to wind through meadowsweet and flag to the loch's edge. The water of the lochs is black with peat. Even now I always think of them as being immensely deep, and during these early visits they seemed bottomless. The brown trout in them are mostly small and very black from the colour of the water, but sometimes you catch one which for no apparent reason has far outstripped its neighbours. But what made the lochs so exciting for us was the fact that at the far end they are drained by a fair-sized stream which winds through peat bog and then hurries down through green meadows between crofters' hay fields to join Loch Etive. Up this burn in the spates of late summer and early autumn run the sea-trout, their presence in the lochs turning for us what would otherwise have been merely a pleasant day's trout fishing into an expedition charged with wild and exciting possibilities. It was as if the mere chance of the presence of these fish had suddenly invested the loch with all the mystery of the tides and currents which each day we could see from the house sweeping down to the Falls of Lora and the Firth of Lorne.

Each day we fished with enthusiasm and endless hope round the shores of every bay and inlet of the lochs, casting to the very edge of the water-lilies and even among the reeds where there was enough open water between the stems to make this possible. We caught many small brown trout and lost many more, for our enthusiasm had not grown tempered with discretion in striking, while often when a rise was seen within reach of us we both cast over it simultaneously, Peter as he untied the tangled lines being appealed to by each side to agree that the blame lay with the other. In this he showed great tact, and his days with us must have tried his patience, for time and again it happened that the rod in the bow had got caught in the lilies at his end and required the boat to be moved towards them, while at the same time that in the stern had become attached to a reed in the opposite direction.

Now and then, especially after rain in the night had filled the little burns and freshened the water of the lochs, there would come a silver grey flash in the black water or a sudden boil and the deep heavy strain on the line which told us that the sea-trout were there. We seldom got many on any one day, but there were few days when we did not at least rise them. But whether we caught sea-trout or not, there was the excitement of fishing in black water frightening in it seeming depth, the dragon-flies over the water-lilies and among the reeds from which the mallard rose, and the thrill of seeing and feeling around us the familiar detail of the Argyllshire countryside.

Sometimes we fished the burn which drained the lochs

to the sea, where the black pools and deep rapid streams running in under overhanging banks belied their promising appearance and produced little else than tiny dark-coloured brown trout even smaller than those in the lochs. One day, however, we fished down to where the stream reaches the salt water, and in a pool near tide level where the water was brackish we were delighted to find our flies taken readily by very lively fish of rather over a quarter of a pound. They were silvery, like sea-trout, and such we assumed them to be. Since then I have realized that we were catching smolts and that for the good of the stream, if not out of consideration for the law, we should have put them back. But in those days we knew no better, and indeed it would have been a hard law which would have denied us the pleasure these little fish gave us as we stood beside the pool where the peaty hill stream first mixed with the clear salt water, in that enchanted no-man's-land where sea and mountain and meadow meet.

On days when the trout in the lochs rose well, we would fish on till late in the afternoon, and on these days by the time we had walked back down the hill road to the house we were glad to rest after tea, in the chintz-covered armchairs of the drawing-room, occupying ourselves with books or tying casts for the next day. But sometimes if we had not gone to the lochs or had come home early, we persuaded our grandmother to let us spend the evening in the bigger row-boat on the sea loch, an act on her part of real unselfishness, for I believe that these evening expeditions were to her a torment of anxiety. Then the versatile Peter was called on again, and armed with long bamboo rods and trailing large red and white flies, we set off to fish for lythe and saithe.

Near the house a short distance offshore lay two little islands, one flat and stony, the other steep and rocky. They were too small to be grazed by the farm stock and consequently were covered with rank grass and meadowsweet in which in spring the gulls nested in hundreds. On the few occasions when I was there in early summer, it was a fascinating ploy to splash out through the seaweed at low water to the nearer of the two, and stumbling across the stony shore and

123

through pink sea thrift to look for nests among the grass, while the gulls and terns hovered and swooped and screamed overhead.

Between the islands if the tide were right, the current ran like a swift river, and here where the dark leaves and branches of the deep-water seaweed waved in the stream lay the lythe and saithe always ready to grab at the trailing flies and giving us a moment of thrill before they were hoisted kicking aboard. In and out and back and across we went, sometimes drifting fast with the current and sometimes battling against it, till Peter was tired and our eyes were so bewitched with watching the moving water that it seemed that the hill and the woods were all sliding down towards Connel and the open sea.

It would be well past our usual bedtime before we had climbed the path to the house, Peter coming behind with the fish which were handed over to the care of a not over-pleased cook who was convinced that lythe and saithe were inedible. Our bedroom windows looked out down the loch, and we would fall asleep, our ears and our sleepy senses filled with the sound of the gulls calling on the islands, while Loch Etive like a huge river swept out to the sea, the great eddies touched by the light in the sky where the sun had gone down behind the hills of Mull.

CHAPTER XII

THE RIVER

LOOKING from Foswell across the broad patchwork expanse of woods and fields which stretched from our own hills to the wall of the Grampians opposite, there was little sign of water. If you knew just where to look, you could pick out here and there a gleam of silver, but those places were few and gave little indication of the river which drained that rich valley. But if after a night of heavy rain you looked back from the hill road on your way to fish the burns, you would often notice the reflection of light on water in unaccustomed places, and as you got higher you might even sometimes see that the flat ground farther to the east had become a great lake as the river rose above its banks and flooded the surrounding farm land.

The valley of the Earn has throughout almost the length of Scottish history marked the dividing line between Highlands and Lowlands, between that part of the country which recognized and supported the established authority of king or parliament, and that other where old loyalties and long-standing feuds lingered on to challenge the authority of the Parliament House of Edinburgh or the Court of St. James. The nature of the river itself shows a mixture of Highland and Lowland characteristics. To look at the burns tumbling down through the rocks and heather and hazel of the glens which lie in the tangle of hills round Loch Earn you would think that you were looking at the head-waters of some strong quick-flowing Highland salmon river, like the Spey or the Dee. For the first few miles of its course east from the loch, streams and shallows and rapids keep the river in brisk and constant motion. But below Crieff the valley broadens and flattens ; the river flows slower and more slowly ; deep still pools and leisurely bends become more frequent than runs and shallows, till by the time it reaches the tidal water below

Perth, it is hard to recognize the stream as the same which miles to the west drains Glen Artney, Glen Lednock and Glen Ogle.

For some years the Earn remained for me little more than a name. I was absorbed by and contented with the burns in our hills which made for me a complete little world, within which was contained all the pleasure, the experience and the possibilities which I could contemplate. Where they passed the point beyond which my fishing did not follow them, the burns passed beyond my ken. I scarcely connected them with the larger streams which one saw on the lower ground below Foswell. Still less did I think of them as part of that deep slow river which one crossed on the road to Perth. Only in the late autumn when the sea-trout came up the burn in our glen did the connection between it and the river become at all real, and even then I think I was apt to accept the happy fact with the minimum of inquiry into its explanation. But after a time Pat began to fish occasionally on part of the Earn which was rented by friends living in the valley, and I went with him.

The piece of water which we fished was some distance up the valley where the Earn was a rather more rapid stream than in the lower stretch with which later we became so familiar. While Pat fished the main streams, often with a big rod, for they were good salmon pools, I fished in great content all the accessible parts of the quiet water under the alder bushes which overhang so much of the Earn's banks. My fishing was not very successful and produced more parr than brown trout, but the deep water in the shade of the bushes seemed full of thrilling possibilities which, had I then known more of the technique necessary for success on the Earn, were in fact far from remote.

Once, on a day when the river was running full and brown, while I was fishing the edge of a deep pool where the flow of the current was slowed by a dyke which crossed the river a short way below, I came on a number of trout rising with quietness and deliberation. They lay at the edge of the deep water, only a few feet from the bank and just beyond

the outer edge of the alder bushes. Only in places where the
bushes were low or in the occasional gaps between them could
one reach the rises, but wherever possible I fished for them
carefully and hopefully in the only way I knew, working my
March Brown and Greenwell's Glory carefully and thoroughly
downstream over them. They treated my flies with indiffer-
ence, sometimes continuing to feed almost beside them, sometimes moving a little way out into the stream, but never rising
to me. These trout tantalized me, for they were bigger than
any I had ever caught, and for long after I thought with
regret of their great slow rises under the bushes. But disappointed and humiliated as I felt, the experience was not
without value, for it showed the obvious need for some new
form of attack if these big trout were to be caught, and led
eventually, when new methods had been learned, to some
measure of success on another part of the river.

Almost directly below Foswell as one looked down to the
valley, the wide expanse of farm land which stretched on
both sides of the river was broken by the solid blackness of a
great wood. Beyond it you could catch one of the rare glimpses
of water which the Earn shows to the surrounding hills, and
here as time went on we went more and more.

The stretch of a river with which a boy first becomes
familiar and on which he gets his earliest experience is likely to
have for him in after years an attraction often out of all relation
to the merits and quality of the fishing which it affords. The
eye of memory is a kindly one. Recollection is more apt to
select and retain the good days than the bad, and the growing
realization that trout rise better on other stretches and other
rivers has little effect on the feelings of loyalty and affection
roused by the memory of the old familiar pools. So it is with
the stretch of the Earn at Aberuthven which we now began to
fish and which in later years I came to know so well. To get
to this part of the river meant quite a long walk, for the main
roads do not approach it and only here and there are narrow
roads leading through farm steadings and then degenerating
into muddy tracks as they struggle on to the old fords which
at intervals cross the river. From where we left the main

road our way led through the big wood to which we had looked down from the hill, and beyond it through great open fields to the waterside. The fields besides the Earn are very large and as we crossed them we would startle big brown hares which, but for our passing, might have remained for days in the deep grass where they lay, undisturbed by anything more alarming than the cattle which fatten on the rich pasture. In early summer the edges of the fields are seldom without pairs of partridges looking the picture of domestic contentment as they quietly pick among the corn or in the young grass, the hen newly off her eggs in the nest among the grass of a near-by sandy bank.

The river flows smoothly and quietly between deep banks in the bed which it has cut in the rich soil, so that you neither see nor hear it till you are almost by its side. The path by which we come to it brings us down to the water's edge at a place where a sloping bed of gravel looks across a smooth-flowing stream to a high bank opposite. Here sand martins fly in and out of the holes which they have made in the sandy face overlooking the rushes and the cuckoo flowers which in June grow close by the water's edge. On the near side the gravel tails off into a little promontory running downstream into shallow water where the current is more rapid. The promontory is a favourite place for the birds, and time and again if we came quietly across the grass field and over the stile on our way to fish, we would find mallard or plover or red-shanks and sometimes all three standing together on the gravel or wading at the edge of the shallow water. Snipe would rise from the soft ground round the mouth of a small stream which here enters the river, and often we disturbed a little group of oyster-catchers which would go off downstream, their cries ringing and echoing over the water, to die away in the distance.

This part of the river was, except in a few places, much more slow-flowing than the upper stretch which we first knew. The trout rose less freely and many of those that did rise were in the deep still stretches where they would seldom look at any fly which we put over them. There were times when even my brother made little of it, and I seldom got more than an

occasional small trout and frequent parr. The regularity with
which we returned empty-handed from the Earn got so mono-
tonous that at last those at home almost ceased to inquire how
we had fared, assuming that we had got nothing unless we
told them otherwise. Looking back on it, I must own that
nowhere have I spent so much time pursuing what I came to
realize was the faintest of hopes as on the Earn at Aberuthven.

For all that, the river was full of interest. One seemed
always on the threshold of some exciting experience. The
possibilities of great trout seemed both infinite and imminent,
and if at moments of weariness and depression during the long
trudge back to the road laden with rods, fishing-baskets and
waders but not with trout, one were tempted to give up all
idea of returning, in a few days the fascination of the river and
the undefeated hope of success had obliterated the memory
of fatigue and disappointment. One saw again the smooth
black water eddying very gently round the old piles which
line the bank, and the rise of a big trout among the shadows
thrown by the alders over the deep holes.

There were big fish in the water, both trout and, later in the year, sea-trout and salmon ; and the deep still pools held more than these. Sometimes on hot days as we passed by the edge of some quiet backwater we would see a long brown shadow fade from view as the pike sank back into the darkness of the deep water. One day in early summer as we walked up the bank of the pool at the upper end of the water, we disturbed a mallard which splashed out from under a willow bush trailing and flapping her wings in the water. She was followed by a string of young ones who took up station in her wake, paddling busily upstream in line-ahead behind her. The end one of the line fell a little behind, and as we looked, a sudden vicious swirl in the water engulfed the little duck which did not reappear. We watched in helpless anger, wishing that we had the means of ridding the pool of what seemed to us an ugly menace.

For several years the Earn trout almost entirely defeated me. Except on rare occasions, the only fish I got were small ones in some of the more rapid streams, the larger ones in the deep pools continuing to disregard the wet flies which I offered them, no matter how carefully I fished, casting the longest line of which I was capable; but the time came when having learned in Hampshire the use of the dry-fly, I came back to Aberuthven to put to the test the growing conviction that now I would have some chance with the big trout in the quiet water.

Morris, the keeper, is one of those who regard trout fishing as a childish but innocent occupation with which those who care may, on rivers where the salmon run late, pass the time till the real fishing starts. While I do not share his view, I cannot feel surprised at the good-natured contempt with which he regarded my early efforts, and after so many weary fruitless days when he watched me fishing down the Aberuthven streams, he had reason to bless the day I first used a floating fly.

Our first real success came on a day in the middle of May many years ago. Public holidays are not as a rule happy in their coincidence with good fishing conditions, but this one was the exception, a fresh day of late spring following rain in the night which had raised the river a few inches and given it a touch of colour. The air was mild, and a light breeze blew upstream. The Earn has a chronic habit of changing its course, cutting into the sand and clay of the banks first on one side and then on the other. As Morris and I walked down the river that morning, we came towards a part where the stream had for the last few seasons been at work eating its way into the deep rich soil on the near side. So a steep bank of clay and gravel fell almost sheer to the edge of the water and from the top of the bank great lumps of turf, undercut by the water, had fallen off into the stream. These lay along the edge of the current and some, more recently fallen, lay only half submerged, making behind them tiny bays of quiet water at the very edge of the fast current. As we came nearer, we saw that the sand martins which nest in the face of the broken bank were flying backwards and forwards low over the stream, constantly swooping to the surface as they picked off the water the olive duns which now we could see rising in quantities from the water or blowing from the bank above.

A few small fish out in the stream were taking the flies with eager splashing rises, but what pleased us most was that trout were feeding quietly and steadily in the smoother patches of water close to the foot of the bank. We made a wide and hurried detour, coming back to the water's edge some yards below the lower end of the stream. Lowering myself over the bank, I got a precarious footing at the edge of the current and faced upstream, while close at my shoulder the sand martins flashed in and out of their nesting-holes. For fifty yards above me, it seemed that each little backwater behind each lump of turf held a trout, and as we watched we would see a nose come quietly up and then a tail appeared as the fish sucked in the olives caught by the eddies and drifted into the quiet water. I had no olives, but a Greenwell did just as well. The light breeze gave all the help one could have wished and if the fly floated even for a few seconds in the smooth water before the current caught the line and dragged it away, it was generally taken. Each trout on being hooked dashed out into the stream and down past me. I could not move back to get below them and some were lost as they were with difficulty brought back up against the current; but most were well hooked, and in the end came to the net which Morris, for once reconciled to trout fishing and as eager as I, handed down from the top of the bank. By the time the top of the stream was reached we had caught nine trout, of which the smallest was not under half a pound, several of them being over one pound.

Such a rise of trout and such a hatch of fly were very much the exception, and it was still to be seen whether the floating fly was effective with the trout which rose spasmodically and often at long intervals in the deep still pools. Above the stream where we fished on that May morning, the river runs over a broad gravelly shallow. On the near side a line of old alder trees grows from the bank and hangs out over the water. There are tall straggly willows, too, beneath which on a spring day you can stand looking up into the blue through a lattice pattern of green leaf and yellow catkin among which the bees move busily. Water hens nest in the bunches of sticks and dead rushes which winter floods have left in the forks of the lowest branches, and from the upper ones pigeons, slipping out as you pass, fly over the water taking as much care to keep the trees between you and them as if your rod were a gun.

Here the stream is very thin and clear, and though trout were often to be seen rising, the shallowness of the water which presents the greatest problem to both the dry- and the wet-fly fisherman, made them almost unapproachable, and we could make little of them. So we seldom tried the shallows— deterred more by the small chance of success than by the knowledge that this particular stream was on the wrong side of the estate boundary which crosses from side to side in a bewildering way.

Above the stream is a deep pool with low willows and stunted alder bushes on the near side. When the river is high, a good current runs down the centre of the pool to lose itself at the foot in a great backwater which eddies round a reed-

covered island where swans nest. Here on calm days good
trout used to rise at intervals, but so far we had tried them
with little success. Only when the water was ruffled by a good
breeze was the surface sufficiently broken to hide the ripple
caused by a wet-fly cast pulled upstream, and during all the
years I have known the Aberuthven water, I have found that
a breeze strong enough to do this is almost fatal to the chances
of finding trout feeding on the surface. It seemed, therefore,
that here was the acid test of the efficacy of the dry-fly at
Aberuthven ; and so it proved.

The Earn valley lying as it does east and west, provides,
like so many of our glens and river valleys, a broad natural
funnel for the wind which in Scotland generally blows out
of one or other of these directions. Down by the waterside the fields are flat and open with few trees and little shelter
of any sort, so that for one who wants still water for fishing
there are not very many days during the summer when he
will find conditions as he would like them. But it often happens that after a day of wind the evening falls calm. For this
reason I formed the habit of going down to the river in the
late afternoon and fishing on into the evening. Reaching
Morris's cottage in the wood between six and seven o'clock,
I would make for the deep pool above the alders, leaving him
to follow if he wished after he had finished his tea—for despite
his contempt for trout, he generally likes to join me at the
river even if fishing fails us and we sit and talk, as we often do,
of grouse and partridges.

On one such evening we found the pool smooth and un-
rippled. A few trout were rising up and down the pool though
the hatch of fly was thin and intermittent, almost negligible by
chalk stream standards. Most of these fish were well out in
midstream where it was not easy to fix their exact position with
relation to objects on the bank, and the long intervals between
rises made this still more difficult. But they were large trout
and were evidently feeding, so we set to work. After much
labour and some disappointment, we found that if the fly
could be brought over them immediately after they had risen
it was generally taken. This meant rapid casting at short

notice, and latterly after gaining some experience of these fish we found that the best way was to keep the fly in the air by constant false casts, ready to make the real cast when the trout was seen to rise, extra line being kept loose in case, as often happened, the trout had moved upstream since his last rise.

It was tiring, but to me fascinating fishing, and the trout were well worth the time and energy spent on them. The largest we ever caught was under two pounds, but there were many of one pound, and the average must have been about three-quarters of a pound. The procedure adopted by these trout varied little. Gradually we came to know it, and once or twice when the light was exceptionally good we were able to see the fish poised vigilant and active just below the surface, moving from side to side, inspecting, eating or rejecting food in the water or on the surface. Unlike chalk-stream trout, their feeding ranged over several yards of water and often more. After each rise they would move rapidly, usually to the side and almost always a little upstream, as if frightened at their own temerity in rising, dropping back after a time to near their starting-point. So it was not surprising that only a fly put over them immediately after the rise to the natural fly had much chance of success. A few moved within still wider limits.

There was one trout near the head of the pool which tried us sorely. He had a regular beat of ten or fifteen yards up which he swam, grabbing flies at long intervals with a savage vigour. It would have been pure chance had one happened to get a fly over him, and in this I never succeeded. I suspected him of being old and bad-tempered. Certainly he was very large.

The strength and condition of these Earn trout were such as I had never before seen equalled, and only in the Don and the Deveron have I since seen any trout to equal them. Certainly they fought better than those of equal size in the chalk streams of the south, and had there been in the pools and streams of the Earn weed beds like those which help the trout of the Itchen in time of trouble, I would have landed very few on the fine gut and small flies which had to be used.

That first success in the calm water of the pool which we know as the Green Bank showed us the possibilities of the quiet water. I remember how keenly I regretted the many days in previous years when I must have wasted similar opportunities and particularly that day with my brother, years before, when under the alders miles up the river, I witnessed but failed to profit by what I now realized to have been an exceptional chance for a dry-fly. I determined that now no similar chances would be missed and that I would try to make up for lost time.

The extravagant hopes often raised in a fisherman's mind by the apparent discovery of new and deadly methods are, luckily both for him and for the trout, rarely justified by subsequent experience, but it is the case that from now on my success on the Earn was greatly increased and Morris's boredom correspondingly reduced. The deep water where the slow current eddied under the shadow of the alder bushes which hitherto I had passed by with scarcely a glance now became the centre of my attention, and by carefully watching Morris and I were able to find good trout rising quietly in many parts of the water. There was a peculiar satisfaction in finding and catching these trout in unsuspected places and often in the face of some difficulty, for the trees and bushes on the Earn are seldom cut to suit the needs of a dry-fly fisherman.

Now, too, we started fishing on late into the evening when the light had begun to fail, and we came to look on the flat glassy calm which sometimes falls on the river as the sun goes down as our greatest opportunity. As evening comes on, the rising trout often move in very near to the shore, perhaps anticipating the big sedges and clumsy moth-like insects which come off the bank in the twilight to flutter and flounder on the surface.

In many of the pools are rows of old piles showing that former proprietors in other days have, like ourselves, found the Earn an unruly changeable stream. Some of the piles are now rotten and moss covered, and useful only as an indication of the height of the water, but for the trout Heaven-sent obstacles round which a cast may be broken or a fly rubbed off. Here, where the tops of the old timbers cause the faintest of eddies in the slow current, the big trout make their leisurely evening meals. Their rises, so close under the shadow of the bank, are, in the failing light, hard to see. Occasionally there comes a great plunge when a sedge flopping on the surface has provoked some big trout beyond endurance ; but generally all you hear is the smallest of sounds no louder than the fall of a big rain-drop, the rise making on the surface a scarcely perceptible movement beside a wooden pile or in line with a bunch of tall grasses leaning over the water. Distances are hard to judge, but sometimes the cast goes right and in that light the chances of a feeding fish taking the fly are considerable.

After a time, even these few rises stop and no sound at all comes from the smooth pool from whose surface little curls of vapour are rising, the first signs of the mist which later will fill the whole valley. Morris and I stop fishing, and after taking down the rod, sit for a time on the bank listening to the quiet of the riverside, resting our tired eyes on the dim blues and greens of the fields and the soft purples of the woods half-seen in the wide valley around us.

CHAPTER XIII

WINCHESTER DAYS

DRY-FLY fishing on chalk streams and the peculiar loveliness of the country and surroundings in which that fascinating sport is enjoyed have all been written of by others possessing infinitely more experience and knowledge than I can ever hope to have. Of Winchester, and the valley of the Itchen in particular, I find it hard to think that there is much which can be profitably added to the pages which Lord Grey wrote over forty years ago. But on looking back over many years of happiness on burn and loch and river, I realize how greatly that happiness has in later years been increased by what was learned on the Itchen, and how incomplete would be any attempt to describe the process of education in fishing which ignored such a powerful and happy influence.

In the winter of 1916 I was at school at the Edinburgh Academy where I had been since the day eleven years before— no less—when, under the care of my two elder brothers, I had made my first timid plunge into the lowest class of the Lower School. That on one of the last days of April 1917 I should be in the London train bound for Winchester accompanied by my cousin, already a Wykehamist, and having among my luggage a brand new iron-bound box of regulation size with my name in large black letters on its lid, was in part due to the war. An unexpected vacancy in the house where my cousin had already been for two years coincided with a sense of restlessness which 1916 and 1917 brought even to a schoolboy and a feeling that eleven years is long enough to spend at even the best of schools ; and so although at sixteen I was considerably above the usual age for entering Winchester, it was finally arranged that I should go there at the beginning of the summer term of 1917.

How greatly my thoughts of Winchester and my wish to go to the school were influenced by what I had heard of its chalk stream it is hard now to recall. Certainly this influenced my thoughts to some extent for I knew that I would have the great good fortune to be given the chance of fishing at times on one of the best-known stretches of that river.

It is not easy to recall with any accuracy the hopes, fears or expectations entertained with regard to places and events prior to seeing or experiencing them. Knowledge subsequently acquired almost of necessity overlays and obscures the re-collection of mental pictures formed in advance, so that it is seldom possible to compare these with the reality. So the full recollection of the picture of a chalk stream which I formed before going to Winchester eludes me. Very probably my expectation was of a fast stream with rapids and broken water, flowing among stones and boulders of chalk. Certainly the picture which fancy painted bore small resemblance to the truth, little as regards the appearance and character of the stream, still less as regards the surroundings through which it flowed.

As the end of the Easter holidays came near, thoughts of fishing receded from my mind, and in their place the thought of the great plunge I was about to take into a new world bulked more and more largely. At no time in my life have I found it easy to achieve that outlook which enables one to " greet the unseen with a cheer." Some, as they grow older, may achieve it, but to few I think is it freely given and seldom, I feel sure, to a boy about to enter for the first time the world of public-school life. The sensations which attend that event are too well-known, and have been too often written of to call for description, and it is not my intention to do more than mention them as the background to that part of the education at Winchester which for me took place in her water meadows and beside her river.

Episodes and experiences in our life acquire, I believe, an added depth and vividness of colouring from the background against which they are set, and looking back on the first three summers during which I fished the Itchen I get the impression that to the newness and strangeness of school life is due in part the intensity of the pleasure which the Winchester fish-

ing gave me and the lasting quality of the influence which
it exerted on my mind.

It has always seemed to me unfortunate that the school
year starts in the autumn. To the alarming experience of his
first term is added for the boy coming to school the depressing circumstances of the time of year. Days are shortening
rapidly. Leaves are falling and drifting forlornly in the
autumn winds, and on playing-fields which only a few weeks
before were made delightful by the sound of the mowing
machine and the smell of cut grass, football pitches have been
marked off and goal-posts put up with their reminders of muddy
games in the failing light of raw winter afternoons.

I was fortunate in escaping this depressing combination of
conditions, and the difficulties inseparable from the opening
weeks at one's first boarding school were made easier by the
beauty of Winchester and the Itchen valley in those last days
of April. The contrast between the climate of Scotland and
England seems never so marked as at that time of year. The
burns and rivers of the north are often then full of snow water
from the drifts on the high hills of which the hard-beaten
residue still lies in the gullies and corries, and the first daffodils
are only newly in flower under trees whose buds are just
opening. But in the south, unless the season be a late one,
the spring is already so far on that summer seems almost at
hand. The trees and the hedges are lightly clothed in fresh
young green, and already beside the chalk streams kingcups
are in flower and fishermen are confidently looking for the
first real hatch of olives, the forerunners of those myriads of
flies which from now on will hatch out in constant succession
all through the summer days.

Those with better memories than my own may be able to
recall whether or not the spring of 1917 was an early one,
but certainly the contrast between north and south that year
seemed to me very marked, and I seemed to be entering
not only a new life but almost a new land. On the railway
embankments and in the deep cuttings in the chalk through
which the line passes between Waterloo and Basingstoke the
profusion of primroses and violets seemed something almost

too good to be true, while the homely sight of Scots firs and
deep heather in the Surrey woods gave me a pleasant feeling
of assurance. I would have been still further comforted had
I then known what I only discovered many years later, that
within little more than a day's walk of Winchester grows the
bog-myrtle which I thought I had left behind me in Scotland.

Railway journeys offer to those who love to watch the
countryside unequalled opportunity of enjoying in imagination
country occupations the thought of which is stimulated by
the scenes through which the train passes. The fox-hunter
selects the jumpable places in the hedges and fences beside the
line ; those who shoot can see in fancy the pheasants breaking
out of tall woods and driven partridges swerving low and fast
over the hedges or crossing high over folds in the Downs. For
the fisherman there is the constant interest of watching burns
and rivers and lochs as he passes and in imagining skilful casts
and rising trout in pools and streams whose appearance is perhaps made more tempting by the brief glimpse which is all he
gets from the train. This last is a sport in which, during train
journeys, I have long indulged, and it was therefore with
surprise and some disappointment that I looked almost in vain
for streams in the hollows and folds of the rolling chalk downland between Basingstoke and Winchester. This elusiveness
and invisibility of the river in the approach to Winchester did
not detract from but rather increased the interest which it held
for me and the excitement with which I first saw it.

In north-country Highland glens the presence of the river
is often apparent both to ear and eye long before one comes
to it, while small tributary streams are constant reminders of
its presence. But in the Itchen valley it is not so, and there
are places where you may follow up the valley close to the
water and yet be unaware of the river's nearness till at the foot
of a meadow you come suddenly on it brimming full, clear and
sparkling, gliding smoothly over the gold and white of its clean
gravelly bed.

During the approach to Winchester by railway there are
few signs of rivers, and none of the Itchen, to be seen, but
it is very different in the town itself. Here, and in those

parts of its outskirts immediately downstream where the daily activities of school life took us, we were seldom without reminders of the presence and importance of the river. Near the low end of the town the High Street crossed its main stream, and every here and there in side lanes and byways you would come suddenly on parts of the stream running strong and clear, washing against the old brickwork of the houses whose walls enclosed it.

In the window of Chalkley's, the fishing-tackle shop which stood at the end of the lime avenue leading to the west door of the cathedral, was the cast of a great trout. This we were assured, with what truth I do not know, had been caught by means of some unspecified bait lowered through a grating in the street into some subterranean part of the stream. A small branch skirted the south end of the cathedral, and after passing through the warden's garden close under the wall of the college, ran on between the sloping grass lawns of our bathing-place to rejoin the main river below. Our walks on Sunday afternoons took us alongside it down by Compton and Shawford, and for some of us the runs round St. Catherine's Hill and past St. Cross in the winter and spring terms were made less tedious by glimpses of its streams and hatches.

The part of the river which we came to know best was the smooth-flowing stream known as Logie which bordered the south side of the school playing-fields, and beyond that stream the water-meadows and winding course of Old Barge, the main river. One of the rougher cricket pitches used by the most junior of the school games to which my lack of athletic talent relegated me in my first term was shrouded in decent obscurity beside the banks of Logie. Here as one lay in the shade of the chestnut trees watching the game, and perhaps secretly hoping that one would not be called on to bat, there was often time to slip off and watch the trout which lay poised and expectant, silhouetted against little patches of sand behind the weed beds.

While those stretches of the river which flowed through the scenes of our everyday activities naturally came to form a familiar part of our lives, the part of the Itchen to which my mind always reverts when I recall Winchester days is that part a few miles above the town stretching upstream from near Martyr Worthy, past the mill at Itchen Abbas and on to near Itchen Stoke. Perhaps it would be unfair to claim for these few miles that they contain the heart of the Itchen valley but certainly one saw here the river at its best, grown almost to its full volume but yet retaining the purity and clearness of a stream lately risen from the deep springs of the chalk downs and not yet spoiled by towns and the works of man.

One of the special charms of fishing is I think that it takes the fisherman among beautiful surroundings, allowing him to spend his days amongst all the natural life and activity of the waterside in a world apart. Woods and plains, hills and the seashore all have their own special plants and flowers and animals for which they form a home, but probably in none of these is the wild life so rich or so concentrated as it is beside a river. Those who make a study of such things tell us that we see only a very little part of the activity which goes on about us in the animal world, our mere presence and the commotion we make as we go on our way, move we never so carefully, disturbing and frightening the animals so that their natural activities are largely suspended till we have passed on.

The more slowly and quietly we move, the more we see of the animal life around us ; for this reason it is probable that, with the exception of the naturalist who moves through the countryside for that sole purpose, no-one has a better chance of seeing intimately the wild life about him than the fisherman. Whether he casts with a heavy rod from the side of a great salmon river, manœuvres his line among hazels and alders on sea-trout water, or is content with the small brown trout of woodland streams or hill burns, he must move quietly ; and nowhere more so than when he watches for rising trout from the banks of a chalk stream. Eye and mind must then be focused and closely concentrated on the detail of stream and ripple, of eddy and waterside immediately about him. If the rise has not yet started he will watch the swifts and swallows for the first signs of the hatch of the flies for which they too wait. When the flies do come he must watch them closely

to decide whether he will try to imitate them with a light or
a blue winged olive, with an orange quill or an iron blue. He
will watch for rising trout round the edges of the beds of water
buttercup and in the eddying water at their downstream end ;
but especially he will watch close in under the banks at either
side where the water reflects in green and gold the shadow
of overhanging water-docken and kingcup. Here the stream
laps the stems of the flags and the roots of rush and meadowsweet where the water hens pick their way and the water rats
move from hole to hole, from waterside to weed bed.

I know of no other occupation and surroundings which
give one such a sense of having gained access to even a small
part of the life and world of the animals as the fishing of
a dry-fly stream in the height of summer. In that delightful
book, *The Wind in the Willows*, in which Kenneth Grahame
writes of the life of the waterside animals the author gives the
chief rôle to the water rat. I do not know whether Mr.
Grahame was a fisherman, but I think few fishermen would
question the claim of the water rat to be the kindly familiar
spirit of the waterside. Whether swimming in the stream, his
body sunk low in the water leaving a little silvery wake as he
passes, whether hopping under the far bank or sitting on his
hind legs as he nibbles at roots and weeds, or deceiving us and
raising false hopes of rising trout as he plops from his hole into
deep water, it is impossible to visualize a dry-fly stream in

the summer days without seeing in fancy that busy friendly little form.

The banks of the Itchen, like those of all the south-country chalk streams which I have seen, housed numbers of water rats, and one day while fishing I came on another of the animal characters of Mr. Grahame's book, the mole. I was crossing a small water-meadow enclosed in a bend of the river a little way below Winchester when on a drier grassy patch surrounded by orchis and beds of campion and meadow-sweet I came on him lying spread-eagled on the grass. I picked him up to see if he were all right. He lay quietly in my hand for a little, and then, when he had sized up the situation, began to push out sideways with a strong swimming motion of his hands and feet. After a time I put him down on the grass, and though there was no vestige of a hole in the ground and little tall growth where he lay, he set to work to force his way down into the grass, and when I left him he had already con-trived partially to hide himself under the few available blades of grass.

It is a curious and delightful attribute of our memories that the countless pictures whose images are impressed on them seem in constant change and motion, so that, depending on our mood or our surroundings, on the season of the year or on other circumstances which we can seldom foretell or control, now one picture and now another comes into focus before the mind's eye. Some recur more frequently than others and there are some of which the focus is unusually sharp and vivid.

Of those memory pictures recorded in my mind I believe that none is more vivid or less affected by the passage of time than that of my first day in the water-meadows at Itchen Abbas. Though this did not occur till several weeks after the beginning of the summer term of 1917, the intervening days had been so full that there had been little time to look round and take complete stock of the new surroundings.

So it was that the morning of late May when I bicycled along the Alresford road past the thatched cottages and gardens of King's Worthy and Martyr Worthy and stood at last at the river's edge in a meadow below Itchen Abbas Mill had all the freshness of a fascinating new experience. The wealth of colour, of flower and plant and animal life in and about the river and the sight in the clear water of rising trout equalling in size the biggest I had ever seen in the north, combined to make me feel, not for the first time but now more intensely than ever before, overwhelmed by happiness. If I could go to Itchen Abbas again after all these years, I could go straight to the spot where, close in under a plant of water-docken growing on the south bank of the stream, I saw my first Itchen trout rise, and probably there would be a trout lying there, for in chalk streams the favourite feeding-places are seldom untenanted.

There is a fascination about these trout which rise quietly close in under the bank. They are often, I think, easier to catch than those in mid-stream, for the bank beside them enables distance to be judged more accurately. But the fascination is not in this. It is in the tiny sound of the rise and the scarcely perceptible movement of the water's surface ; in the brown form and the waving tail barely seen in the green shadow against the trail of weed moving below the surface ; in the flag bending low over the stream where the trout lies poised ; in the water rat or the reed warbler moving near by. That part of me which took pleasure in catching trout among the rushes and meadow-sweet of the smallest pools of Perthshire burns found an equal happiness in the sight of these much larger fish whose movements in the stream seemed to form a natural part of the rich riverside life about them.

If the Itchen Abbas water was the heart of the Upper Itchen valley, the central point of that stretch was the road bridge which crossed the river at Itchen Abbas Mill. Here the river falling from the level of a deep slow stretch of water above rushed through the mill hatches down into the big hatch hole below. When the hatches were open a strong rush of white and broken water swept down through the centre of the pool, while at either side were deep back-waters where the smoother water reflected the reeds and flags which grew tall along the water's margin. At the tail of the pool the stream broadened and shallowed, the water lost the cloudy greenness which depth gives to chalk streams, and flowed clear and sparkling over clean chalky gravel. Then it passed under the road bridge to spread out below into the wide shallow stream which we knew as the Broad Meadow, perhaps the best of all the excellent meadows on the Itchen Abbas water.

The pool below the hatch was full of big trout, but those in the back-waters at either side were hard to catch in the swirling water where eddies caught the line and made the fly drag almost as soon as it lighted on the surface. In the shallower rippling water at the tail of the pool trout were constantly to be seen, their backs and tails showing above the surface. The sight of such big fish evidently feeding steadily and persistently was tempting and hopeful, but in fact these fish were nearly all feeding on shrimps in the sand and gravel and weeds of the stream's bed, and though we often fished for them it was only now and then that one raised its head to notice a fly floating on the surface.

Later, when I became familiar with Schubert's songs, the melody of the first song in the cycle of the *Maid of the Mill* never failed to bring back to me the memory of the mill at Itchen Abbas. I would picture the young apprentice miller dreaming on the road bridge over which I have so often leant while the water hurries and ripples on to wander through the green water-meadows of the lower Itchen valley, past Winchester to the growing bustle of Eastleigh, and so at last out into the wide busy world of Southampton Water.

The chalk streams of the south possess a characteristic seldom to be seen in the streams of the north—a tendency to split up into several branches, some of which wander a considerable distance from the main river. It is very marked on the Test, the Itchen and the Kennet, and there can be few stretches of those rivers where one can say without hesitation that what appears to be the main channel does in fact carry the whole stream. It is a pleasant habit, and I like to think of these little side streams wandering off on their own devices to explore the sides of the valley, perhaps straying as far afield as the edge of the wood which borders the water-meadow where you may come on them unexpectedly, rippling along, overhung with bramble and shaded by willow.

Man has encouraged and turned to account this characteristic. In the true water-meadow you will find the side streams divided and sub-divided into little streamlets led through the meadow to freshen and irrigate the grass. The sides of each little stream are marked by a luxuriant growth of lush grass, kingcup and forget-me-not, whose vivid green frames and emphasizes by contrast the sparkle and clearness of the water flowing over its gravel bed of white and gold. Some of these irrigation ditches in the meadows round Winchester were too small to hold trout, but all the real side streams held them. Where paths crossed them it was always worth while to look carefully over the edge of the bridge at the downstream end where the trout liked to lie, their tails just visible and their heads under the shelter of the bridge.

To me there is a great attraction about the small stream and the unexpected pool, and I am apt to value the trout caught in such a place more highly than his larger neighbour killed on the main stream. Just above the bridge at Itchen Abbas Mill such a side stream rejoins the river. It branches off the main river half a mile above, and flows first under trees and then through a thicket of tall reeds and willows. Only at odd places can it be approached, but it is possible to push one's way up for a little distance from its lower end. This I sometimes did, tempted by the sight of big fish feeding in the channel between the weed beds which in places choked and narrowed it to a mere ribbon of open water. Once, keenness overcame discretion and took me to a point where I could only with difficulty get any foothold in the perilously soft ground which bordered the stream, while the reeds were so high that only by holding the rod at the full length of my arm was it possible to keep the cast clear of their tops. When at length I reluctantly turned back I could see more trout rising still farther ahead safe from all possible approach, some of the many which in the quiet and remote side streams of the Itchen, as in those of other chalk streams, will feed and fatten and die in untroubled security far from the reach of the fisherman.

147

I have written more of the circumstances and surroundings of the Winchester fishing than of its results, but while the former, rightly and happily, have a large place in my recollections of these days, the latter were by no means negligible. Turning to the fishing register which for a few seasons at that time I kept, I see that in 1917, fishing with Lord Grey, I caught eight trout averaging one pound. The number of days I fished at Itchen Abbas that year is not recorded, but probably I was there three times during this first summer. This was, I think, practically the last summer during which Lord Grey was able to fish with a dry-fly, and even then he was fighting a losing battle against the fast-growing handicap of failing sight, to the great concern of the old fisherman at Itchen Abbas who wanted him to try some curious and unlikely cure, the details of which I have forgotten.

In the summer of 1918 I fished there either alone or in the company of my Wykehamist cousin, and in three days of that summer we got eighteen trout. On the second of these days, the 30th of June, the Itchen showed for our benefit one of the peculiar and most attractive attributes of the chalk stream. Heavy rain had fallen in the night, culminating towards morning in a torrential downpour through the last of which my cousin and I bicycled along the Alresford road. The sun came out before we reached Itchen Abbas, but the trees were still dripping, while along the sides of the road ran little torrents of water, thick and opaque with chalky mud. Our hopes were near zero, for to us, accustomed to the behaviour of Scottish burns and rivers in similar weather, it seemed certain that the river would be hopelessly thick and unfishable, and that we should be cheated of a day to which we had looked forward so eagerly. But when we had left our bicycles at Lord Grey's cottage and had hurried down through the meadow in front of it, we found the river clear, sparkling and lovely as ever, reminding us that the water now flowing past us was risen from depths in the chalk far beyond the reach of the heaviest rain to spoil its clearness. That day, the record of which is heavily underlined in my fishing register, the trout rose better than usual, and though we had no net with us, and must have lost several of which I have neither record nor memory, I see that we caught eight trout of which the largest was one and three-quarter pounds.

The following summer, my last at Winchester, we fished on four days at Itchen Abbas and got thirty-five trout all over a pound, the limit below which we did not kill them. Of these, the two largest weighed two pounds and two pounds five ounces, and I see I have recorded that the best fly was the Red Quill. This fly seems to be regarded by some of the more modern writers on dry-fly fishing as old-fashioned and no longer very effective, but to my knowledge the trout in Scotland at least do not so regard it, and if I ever fish the Itchen Abbas water again I shall use it.

Of the four days on which I fished during this summer two were in the nature of windfalls. The annual cricket match between Eton and Winchester was to be played at Eton, and the whole school was allowed a long week-end to go to watch it. Now, while I am no cricketer, I find it very pleasant in hot summer weather to sit under trees at the edge of a well-kept cricket field watching the game played in lovely surroundings, and when the interest of a keenly contested school match is added the prospect is one to which, normally, one would look forward with eagerness. But no fisherman who had once seen the crystal stream of the Itchen at Itchen Abbas, the sway and bend of the reeds, the white stars of the water buttercups, and the quiet rise of trout under the banks and round the weed beds would, if he had the opportunity, hesitate to do as I did. Travelling to London to make the deception complete, I caught the first train back from Waterloo. I put up at the old half-timbered inn in Winchester High Street which is called the " God Begot House," and bicycling out each morning to Itchen Abbas I spent there two of the happiest fishing days of my life, troubled but little by the qualms of conscience and free even from the need to hurry back for " Names Calling," a freedom which allowed me to enjoy for the first time the evening rise on the Itchen.

Pleasant as the time at Winchester was, and certainly the light in the picture far exceeds the shade, the long absences in the south made one long for Scotland, and appreciate it during the holidays perhaps more even than one had done before. At the start of each term we used to get hold of Bradshaw, and from it work out in detail the journey north, deciding by which train we would travel three months hence and dwelling with delight on the names of the familiar north-country stations. As the end of term approached the sense of anticipation became very real. Those who lived in the north were given what was called " Scots Leave," being allowed away a day earlier than the rest, a privilege which added greatly to the pleasure of the end of term and the thrill of the journey.

The journeys were indeed not without their adventurous side. Those were the days of the first serious Zeppelin air attacks on London, and sometimes our passage through the city coincided with a raid. Once we spent an exciting night sitting in a blackened train in Wimbledon station while a raid went on over London, and the next day travelled north in a train crowded beyond what seemed possible with what must have been some of the very first evacuees. But such excitements were exceptional, and as a rule our journeys were peaceful, though made thrilling enough for us by the mere fact of their northward direction.

Euston was our usual starting-point, a Euston so different from that at which we had arrived at the beginning of term as to be hardly recognizable. In actual fact the arrival and departure platforms bear a dissimilarity which has always seemed to me scarcely to be accounted for by the different hours at which they are commonly seen. Even now when Euston has become a more familiar and prosaic place than in the Winchester days I half-believe that there are two stations, one reserved for the happy people going north, and one for the harassed and unshaven, hurrying late for meetings, appointments or connections, from the incoming train. The very porters seemed different if one were north-bound, and one I remember especially, a Perth man who, gauging our sentiments and weaknesses, found it profitable to expand to us of his native land, assuming an accent perhaps more marked than that with which heredity and upbringing had endowed him.

In those days we always travelled sitting up in third-class carriages, and indeed had I been offered the most luxurious sleeper, it is doubtful whether I should have accepted it for fear of falling asleep and so missing some of the thrill of the journey —moonlight on a summer's night over the home counties, with mist in the hollows and rising from canals and rivers, and along hedgerows the great shapes of elm and oak, their dark outlines softened by a silver haze ; Crewe at 2.30 a.m., and dawn soon after ; the light growing as we started to climb up the valleys and past the grey stone dykes of Cumberland ; then the full day as we wound our way among the soft green folds of the hills of Dumfriesshire and Lanarkshire.

" Time," wrote George Russell, the Irish poet, " is a swift winnower." It sifts the good from the bad, that which is light and of little account from what has substance and weight and permanence. So it is with our recollections. As time goes on, those impressions which are mere passing ones and which have made on our minds no deep imprint, tend, though they may never be quite obliterated, to recede from consciousness. Then more and more there emerge sharp and distinct those mental pictures which contain the lasting memories which in future we shall have always with us.

The memory of Winchester contains for me many such pictures, partly perhaps by reason of the strong light and shade of those war days which tend to throw into relief the recollection of places and events ; but mainly, I think, because my memories of the place are chiefly associated with the surroundings in which our school life was lived—and these could hardly have been more lovely. " Meads " on a summer day and its line of big elms, the chestnuts on the banks of Logie with St. Catherine's Hill beyond ; the lime avenue leading to the west door of the cathedral ; everywhere the flint walls where wall-flower had rooted and flourished in the crumbling cement, and wistaria hung from the coping—and above all the river.

I have in another place * tried to tell more of the Itchen

* By Many Waters

Abbas water, and what I owe of happiness to it and to Lord Grey who gave me those days of such pleasure; but of all the infinitely varied forms of beauty with which Nature surrounds and delights us there can be few more difficult to describe with any approach to adequacy than that which she scatters in profusion along the banks of a chalk stream.

The older we grow, and the more we see of the world in which we live, the more do we realize that Nature's store of beauty is inexhaustible in a way far beyond our comprehension. That one form of it should appeal more keenly than another to the taste and imagination of the individual is inevitable. To claim for that form superiority over another would be little less than irreverence, but the fisherman who has seen in summer the water-meadows and the chalk streams of Hampshire knows at least that thenceforward his memories will be greatly and permanently the richer.

THE END

PRINTED IN GREAT BRITAIN AT
THE PRESS OF THE PUBLISHERS